THEATRE CLASSICS FOR THE MODERN READER

To reproduce the values and effects of the theatre on the printed page is the ambitious aim of this series of the classics of the stage. Although good plays have always been read as well as acted, few playwrights before the era of Ibsen and Shaw have ever written with any public other than the theatre audience sharply in their minds. In consequence, the reader of older plays is usually required to supply his own visualizing of the staging and his own interpretation of stage action and even the manner of the delivery of the lines themselves. Frequently he is also required to put up with abbreviations and other space-saving printing devices.

This modern reader's edition of theatre classics vitalizes the outstanding plays of the past with the kind of eye-pleasing text and the kinds of reading and acting guides to which today's reader is accustomed in good published editions of twentieth century dramas. The text itself has not been altered except for occasional modernizations of spelling and punctuation (common to all modern editions of earlier works) and the rare use of italics for emphasis when the reading of a line is not immediately clear. Essentially, that is, the author's text is as he wrote it. Added to it are descriptions of scenes and costumes, indications of expression and action, and explanation of words and references not readily comprehensible.

The illustrations should aid immeasurably in visualizing the play. A description of the original staging, stage conditions, and stage techniques is provided partly as still another aid to visualization but principally to show how the playwright adapted his materials to suit the particular stage conventions of his time. Companioning each play are also a sketch of the author's life, an analysis of the play, and a selective bibliography to make this as much an all-in-one edition as possible.

The Rivals

RICHARD BRINSLEY SHERIDAN

The Rivals

EDITED BY

**VINCENT F. HOPPER and
GERALD B. LAHEY**

New York University

WITH A NOTE ON THE STAGING

GEORGE L. HERSEY

Bucknell University

ILLUSTRATIONS BY
FRITZ KREDEL

BARRON'S EDUCATIONAL SERIES
Woodbury, New York

The Rivals

THE PLAYWRIGHT

From a literary standpoint, it is difficult to determine what should be said of Sheridan's life: for of his four careers (that of playwright, that of manager and part-owner of the Theatre Royal, Drury Lane, London, that of Parliamentary Member for Stafford and prominent Whig, and simultaneously a scintillating career as man of fashion and intimate friend of the First Gentleman of Europe) the first was over when Brinsley was little more than twenty-five. The others had hardly begun.

If Sheridan had died at the age of thirty, we should have mourned in him the premature loss of great fertility of wit and facility of invention and speculated on what he might have done had he lived to become an ancient like Shaw. The grief would have been vain: after his brilliant wooing of the comic muse, Sheridan immediately and almost completely abandoned her for other blandishments. For if Sheridan had died at the fall of the curtain on his highly successful burlesque *The Critic* in October of 1779, his literary reputation would stand just where it is.

Actually it was his dazzling, early conquest of the comic stage that enabled Sheridan to get control of the Drury Lane theatre; and it was the control of the theatre that enabled him to pay for the expensive election contests that made him a member of the House of Commons and the valued friend of the ravishing Duchess of Devonshire, Lady Bessborough, Mrs. Crewe, etc. As Whig politician and man of fashion, he bears some resemblance to his own Charles Surface: a man of endless gaiety, wit, and charm,—and debts. Like Oscar Wilde, all who met him found him one of his own best "productions." And like Surface, his gaiety flared up most brightly in adversity: we have the stories of his having to rent for an evening's entertainment of friends his own

9

plate and china from the pawnbroker in whose more or less permanent custody it was. His theatre burned down in 1809 and was rebuilt again more imposingly despite lack of insurance. On the night of the fire, the ominous glare was visible through the windows of the House of Commons where Sheridan was scheduled to speak. On learning that his own theatre was in flames, he went to a neighboring tavern and, calmly ordering his drink, inquired whether a man might not have his glass of wine at his own fireside.

As for the Sheridan family history, it is as full of caprice and paradox as his career. In a sense he came naturally by his literary and stage interests: his mother Frances Sheridan was a moderately successful writer of novels and plays. Sheridan's celebrated Mrs. Malaprop was faintly anticipated in the character of Mrs. Tryfort in his mother's comedy *Journey to Bath*. His father, Tom Sheridan, an actor, had a limited success as theatremanager in Smock Alley, Dublin. Later he was a fairly successful teacher of elocution in England. Richard Brinsley's grandfather, another Tom, a schoolmaster and scholar, was a friend of the great Swift. Hence Sheridan's verbal dexterity would seem naturally come by. However, the family history does not record progenitors remarkable for graceful and lively wit. Indeed the clerical grandfather lost a preferment by a particularly inept sermon delivered on the anniversary of the Hannoverian succession on the text "Sufficient unto the day is the evil thereof." Dr. Johnson, the literary dictator of his day, had said of Sheridan's father that he was "dull, naturally dull; but it must have taken him a great deal of pains to become what we now see him; such an excess of stupidity, Sir, is not in nature."

Regardless, in no part of Sheridan's life or personality does one find dullness. His life reads almost like the script of an over romantic musical comedy or light opera. Before he was twenty-one, he had participated in two duels and managed a romantic elopement to France with Miss Elizabeth Ann Linley; before he was thirty he had written two of the liveliest comedies in English, one of the best farces, and one of the best light operas. For over a quarter of a century he was one of the most brilliant figures in a Parliament that contained Pitt, Fox, and Burke. And his speech against Warren Hastings, lasting over five and a half hours and delivered with rapid stacatto brilliance without notes, achieved a reputation almost mythical in grandeur; it was regarded by competent members of the Parliament as exceeding in magnificence any comparable utterance in history. Even in the declining days of a life well saturated with port and claret, brandy and water, he could hold the critical Lord Byron spellbound by his conversation from six in the evening until midnight had passed. And even in his last days of poverty and penury, even then he was colorful in the squalor of his fall, with the officers of the law ready to carry his expiring frame to the debtor's den for debts. Johnson must have been right: the father's dullness must have been an acquired and hence not a transmittible trait: Brinsley inherited none of it.

Like his own sprightly Charles Surface, Sheridan managed to combine gallantry, gaiety, and gambling. His personal attractiveness enabled him to win the affections of Miss Linley, a beautiful and gifted daughter of a family that was apparently designed by Thomas Mann, so evident in it was the affinity of disease and precocious musical talent. All of the many children of the family were personally endowed with rare musical talent and personal beauty and were particularly susceptible to tuberculosis. The exquisite voice and fragile beauty of Sheridan's wife early succumbed to the tuberculary scourge. Sheridan then married in his forties a slip of a young thing, Hester Jane Ogle, barely twenty and daughter of a Dean of Westminster; it was she who remained devoted and faithful to Sherry despite his own amorous driftings, sharing with him at the end illness and misery. At that point, Sheridan was his own Charles Surface in reverse, all his personal effects being sold to stave off creditors so that he might stiffen at last in a rented room.

Sheridan was born in that cradle of writers of English comedy—Dublin, birthplace of Wilde and Shaw likewise. His life describes a brilliant arc rising from the poverty of 12 Dorset Street, Dublin, and passing like a meteor across the London horizon to sink into the poverty of 14 Savile Row; he was born in October of 1751 and died in July of 1816. It was a half century of events that shook mankind, and Sheridan was everywhere in touch with his time. Yet, in spite of Sheridan's brilliant personal success during the full tide of his career, the eighteenth century was aristocratic, and Sheridan's imposing friends always spoke of him as of low or humble origin. Walpole, for example, spoke of him as "the son of an Irish player," and his official biographer and countryman, Tom Moore, speaks of his "disadvantages of birth and station." Watkins, the memoralist, refers to him as one having neither "pedigree nor property." Actually, the Sheridans were gentry, of good family, with bishops and royal secretaries in the family history. But their gentility was somewhat legendary by 1751, and however good a defense of it by Sheridan's mother Frances in her *Memoir,* unless family bestowed privilege and property, rank and connection, it was of merely sentimental value; Sheridan's family gave him only intelligence and vigor to which he added great charm of manner.

More need not be said of Sheridan's family than that poverty drove them to England; from England they took refuge temporarily in France from importunate creditors, leaving Richard Brinsley, however, to be educated at Harrow. Despite the fact that two of the plays of Sheridan's mother were produced by Garrick at Drury Lane in 1763, debts drove the family cross channel to France in 1764. Richard had been entered at Harrow in 1762, the Sheridans being acquainted with Dr. Sumner, the headmaster of the famous foundation. Biographers in general agree in saying that he was unhappy there (he stayed for about six years) at a most impressionable period of a young boy's life. He was evidently made conscious of the fact that he was the son of

a poor player who had already strutted and fretted
his hour upon the stage; he often felt depressed and
dispirited, insignificant and neglected; the experience
left him perhaps with a permanent sense of insecurity
and social inadequacy, of sensitivity to status. Thirty-
five years after he had left Harrow, he still recalled the
place with gloom. Lady Holland (and some others),
who rather specialized in the slightly malicious detec-
tion of the weaknesses of others, gave it as her opinion
that Sheridan's desire to rise in the world of politics, to
become a great Parliamentary orator and political figure, was owing to a desire to compensate for the hum-
bleness of his origins; his experience at Harrow lends
some basis to support the view. Lady Holland also
offered it as her view that his desire to take his place in
the world of literature and fashion (as an intimate of
the Prince Regent, for example), his gallantries, his in-
fidelities to his two wives, was mainly owing to a vanity
which was compensating for a sense of deficient pedigree in the great world of Whig fashion and magnificence.

He rejoined his family at Bath on their return from
France in 1770. Whatever the psychic scars he bore
away with him from Harrow, he did become a middling
student of the classics although contemporaries felt him
slightly undereducated by gentlemanly standards; that
is to say, he substituted brilliance and vivacity for sobriety and gravity. Moreover, he did acquire a taste
for reading and literary style; despite his own great
oratorical success, he was better at Horace and Virgil
than Demosthenes; he knew much of the poet Spenser
and thoroughly admired Dryden. Indeed his own pre-
carious hold on scholarship may have sharpened his wit
and imagination for the conception of such figures as
Mrs. Malaprop. Moore, his official biographer, tells us
that Sheridan was never quite sure of his spelling, when
to double his consonants, for example. Perhaps the
phonetic vagaries of Mrs. Malaprop have their counter-
part in the orthographic ones of her creator. Whatever

his scholarly success at Harrow, the acquired prima donna temperament, the touchy sense of pride is important to his biographers. (Is Faulkland of *The Rivals* an externalization of this sensitive edge of his temper?) For if, as Lady Holland avers, it launched Sheridan into the sunny waters of comic drama, it also led him to abandon the craft. Rapidly successful at literary comedy (all of his brilliant comedy appeared between 1775 and 1780), Sheridan was determined to establish himself in the world of politics and fashion. For Sheridan realized that although England's aristocrats allowed artists to associate freely with them, this privilege was never to be mistaken for an acceptance as equals. And such was Brinsley's pride that an equal or the "role" of an equal would alone satisfy him.

After a political career of over thirty years, Sheridan told Creevey in 1805 that the happiest day of his life was that on which he was first elected to Parliament as the Member for Stafford. The romantic Shelley wrote (apparently with pride) that great authors, poets in particular, were the "unacknowledged legislators" of mankind. Sheridan, for all of his capricious, irresponsible, quixotic temper, was an eighteenth century man, not a romantic; he fully intended to achieve status by becoming one of the publicly acknowledged legislators of mankind, a situation which would allow him to move in the fashionable and fabulous Whig world with something like equal dignity. Hence he used his early literary success to acquire control of the policy and property of the Drury Lane theatre so that with the proceeds and profits of this venture he could pay his heavy election costs and fulfill his social duties. For about thirty years the theatre was to support the aspirations and activities, political and social, of Sheridan. It was mainly in connection with this theatre and its financing, reading its manuscripts, paying its actors, that Sheridan acquired his notorious reputation for procrastination and irregularity, for picturesque undependability. However, the business enabled him to remain a prominent Foxite

Whig for more than a quarter of a century, always a vigorous member of the Opposition. Perhaps then, as Lady Holland suggested, it was his sensitive pride that led him to seek a more elevated status and become one (to paraphrase Goldsmith on Burke)

Who, born for the theatre, at too early an age

To Party gave up what was meant for the stage.

We today cannot help thinking that there is more of interest in his literary comedies than in his Parliamentary utterances, which have indeed something of the theatrical, meretricious-sublime about them. Especially when Sheridan was seeking solemn elevation of sentiment, his oratory reads a little like the artificial flights of a Surface; Sheridan was, however, at his best in Parliament when the occasion required satiric ridicule and witty exposure of fraud and falseness. Then his oratory has the authentic literary ring about it. But although *meretricious* may possibly apply to his quality of utterance at moments, it never touched the quality of his motives. During this period when everywhere in Europe and England aspirations were awakening for independence and a higher status for the common man, Sheridan's pride forebade his taking up with the increasingly numerous Tory reactionary personalities and the rewards therefrom. Burke, for example, did not scruple to get cash and sinecure from his titled masters; Sheridan scrupulously avoided even the shadow of a suspicion of being for sale, even in those easy days. Neither a place nor a pension seeker, he always had about him the quixotic gesture of one who wore the poor-but-proud panache.

Perhaps a few more details about Sheridan, especially about his domestic and business personality, will suffice before considering the qualities of our particular play. His first wife was Elizabeth Ann Linley, the Bath nightingale, whose ethereal beauty and exquisite voice charmed everyone in England from the royal couple to the average chairman. She was the object of the flattering attentions, of the obsessions of men of all ages and ranks. She had already made the conquest of one rich middle-aged man, Walter Long, by the time she was sixteen. Already by 1771 a play, *The Maid of Bath,* had been written about her and the obsessive attachments which she inspired. Hence she had fame and unwelcome notoriety before she was twenty. She so captivated another elderly admirer that his oppressive attentions led to her elopement to France with Richard Brinsley Sheridan as her chivalrous protector. Parental intervention at length led to their return, and eventually they were wed for a second time, there being some doubt as to the validity of their French marriage. Sheridan's gallantry during this harassed period of Eliza's life, his chivalrous defense of her against Captain Mathews' offensive aggressiveness involved him early in two very fierce duels and gave him some practical insight into the Acres-O'Trigger scenes of *The Rivals.* And his conduct won for him forever the toast of the beaux, Miss Linley. In 1773, Elizabeth wrote to Brinsley that it was "not your person that gained my affection. No, Sheridan, it was that delicacy, that tender compassion . . . which induced me to love you." There was something of a rarefied Miss Lydia Languish in Elizabeth.

It was on April 13, 1773 that they were married for the second time at Marylebone church in London. When two days later the *Morning Post* announced that "Mr. Sheridan, a student of the Temple, is at last firmly united to the Maid of Bath, on Tuesday last," it was optimistic in the use of the adverb "firmly." Sheridan did not have a domestic temperament; he found it difficult to "settle down," but we are glad to believe with Lady Holland that his amorous digressions were products of social vanity, not personal vice. Even Eliza's deep devotion was at length weakened; in 1790 they were temporarily estranged by his inconstancies. Mrs. Sheridan had for a moment Candida's temptation; she said later of this period that had the royal Duke of Clarence been ten years older than he was, she might have yielded to his importunities to run away with him.

Again biographers have hinted that her daughter was the child of Lord Edward Fitzgerald, a result of a liaison contracted during despondency at her Sherry's waywardness. Perhaps this is one of the publications of the Scandal Club. At any rate, on her death, Sheridan realizing his own primary culpability could assert only that she was an angel. Indeed, Maria's devoted, faithful patience waiting for Charles Surface's reform has in it a hint of Eliza's plight.

But Sheridan's life was not as sentimental as his comedy. Within three years of her death, Sheridan had married again; in his second marriage he assumed the role which he had ridiculed in Sir Peter Teazle, his bride, a buoyant twenty, and Brinsley a bottle-worn forty-three. However, he was still the incorrigible husband despite a complexion now ablaze with the consequences of steady drinking; the heart still wandered, and his Hester Jane Ogle—Mrs. Sheridan II—shared her husband with other beauties who wandered through the lustrous chambers of Devonshire, Burlington, or Carleton Houses. The second wife, daughter of the Dean of Winchester, perhaps offered Sherry in social position, and hence security, what the first wife offered in beauty and talent.

From the standpoint of his career, 1775 was the marvellous year in Sheridan's life. At the beginning of it, he was known only as the young husband of the beautiful Eliza; at the end, he was being celebrated as the writer of two of the best comedies in the English language. In 1774, he had written to his father that he was at work on a comedy for Mr. Harris of Covent Garden Theatre. It was produced as *The Rivals* in January of 1775. Not immediately successful, it was withdrawn from the stage and subjected to serious revision. Unlike Shaw, who in his day determined to re-educate his audience, Sheridan conformed quietly to the taste of his house, carefully observing the criticisms levelled against his original text and purging it of heaviness. The eleven days of his revision were among the most important of his life. The revised play was immediately popular and the hit of the season; Sheridan's name quickly became a token of brilliance. In November of the same year, Harrison produced for him *The Duenna,* a repository (economically enough) of many of the verses he had written for Eliza during his courtship; it was a sort of light opera, dialogue interspersed with songs, the music composed by his father-in-law Linley. It was also a triumph. In record for continuous performance it outdistanced the famed *Beggar's Opera*: forty years later Lord Byron still could not praise it too highly. The song-books made from it were as profitable as the theatrical presentation. Sheridan had had two great successes within a twelve month period.

As a result, the young husband now had enough money to support his wife and family. Actually, Eliza was quite willing to continue her highly lucrative career as a public singer. But Sheridan's quixotic pride forbade. Many people at the time felt that for a woman to expose herself to the public gaze was to diminish the glow of her maiden modesty; stage and screen celebrities have since learned to control this girlish shyness. But Sheridan wished that his wife should never appear as a paid public entertainer. And the success, the two successes of the year, made his wish practicable. With the enormous popularity of both productions, Sheridan found himself at little more than twenty-four a man who had arrived. Even Dr. Johnson (finding him in no sense as dull as the father) was moved to sponsor him for membership in the famed Literary Club, remarking, "He who has written the two best comedies of his age is surely a considerable man." Among the members were Gibbon, Burke, Fox. It was with Fox that Sheridan was to connect his political fortunes and future; perhaps the Literary Club was the original staging ground of his political career.

At any rate, Sheridan's success as a playwright enabled him to turn both socially and economically to grander enterprise. Between 1776 and 1778, succeeding to the great Garrick, Sheridan acquired control of the property and policy of the Drury Lane theatre. His financial manipulations in acquiring the structure and its patent defy the analysis of either contemporaries or historians. Obviously the prodigal and practically impecunious Sheridan had a knack for finance as elusive and complicated as that of Joseph Surface for moral and social situations. From this point on, his economic life crawled through an underground labyrinth of mortgages, borrowings, interest, credit, profits, payments that would have utterly baffled the simple gossips of the Scandal Club. It was Byron's opinion that Sheridan had handled everybody's money but his own. As a business man his name became a symbol for procrastination, irregularity; but his tactfulness and charm, his ingenuity and improvisation expanded to cover his impracticality, and for more than a quarter of a century, the Drury Lane theatre continued to support Sheridan's adventures into the fashionable life of London. Of course, it should be added that as Member of Parliament he was immune to arrest for debt. When after more than a quarter of a century in the House of Commons, he finally lost his seat, he was promptly in real difficulties for his endless arrears.

But unlike his own Charles Surface, Sheridan was not ultimately rescued from misfortunes and reckless prodigality of spending by a benevolent uncle returning from India. Rather, as his days drew to a close, his portraits by Gainsborough and Reynolds (even the noted one in which his wife represented St. Cecelia) were auctioned to pay part of his debts; finally the bailiff and sheriff were waiting to pick up the sick, broken man in bed and blanket to carry him off to the sponging house for indebtedness. Lord Byron's spoken epitaph for that forlorn figure was "poor dear Sherry, what a wreck is that man!" Ironically, despite the shabbiness and neediness of his last days, Sheridan was laid to rest in the poets' corner in Westminster Abbey; the poor player's son had as honorary pall-bearers royal dukes, earls, bishops, lords.

Sheridan is well summed up in a contemporary review of Tom Moore's *Memoirs of Sheridan*: "He . . . was for thirty years the most brilliant talker—the greatest conversational wit of the splendid circle in which he moved . . . Sheridan's conceptions . . . seem always to have flowed from him with great copiousness and rapidity. But he had taste as well as genius—and ambition as well as facility, . . . his labour . . . not in making what was bad tolerable, but in making what was good, better and best."

THE PLAY

First Performance: January 17, 1775

Excerpts from the *Morning Post* of January 19: . . . *the* Rivals, *at Covent Garden, is withdrawn for the present, to undergo some severe prunings, trimmings, and patchings, before its second appearance.*

Second (Revised) Performance: January 28, 1775

Excerpt from the *Morning Chronicle* of January 28-31: *The cuttings have been everywhere judicious.*

The Rivals is a specimen of the perennial comedy of impersonation or mistaken identity. The vitality of this kind of farcical situation is evident in its longevity, stretching from Jonson and Shakespeare through Congreve, Goldsmith, Sheridan to Oscar Wilde's *Lady Windermere's Fan* and *The Importance of Being Earnest* to Shaw's *Arms and the Man* and *Major Barbara*.

Sheridan's work is especially reminiscent of Goldsmith's anti-sentimental comedy *She Stoops to Conquer,* performed successfully only two years previously. *The Rivals* might have been called, not too fancifully, *He Stoops to Conquer* since its main plot revolves about a potentially rich young Captain, son to a baronet and entertaining expectations of £3000 a year, who is under the necessity of masquing himself in the guise of a half-pay ensign in order to satisfy the ticklish sensibility of Lydia Languish. In Goldsmith's play, Kate Hardcastle, the daughter of country gentry, felt constrained to adopt the guise of barmaid and poor cousin in order to entrap the eccentric and skittish personality of Young Marlowe.

21

The two plays have a further similarity in that each one
has a secondary plot, involving another young couple
who are aware of the deception but do not reveal it.
Captain Absolute, indeed, refers to his emergence from
his *alias* as a return to his "more elevated character,"
implying that, like Kate, he has been stooping.

We do well to remain content, nevertheless, with the
present title, for it suggests not only the rivalry of Absolute with his other self Ensign Beverly but likewise with
the amiable rustic of Clod Hall, Bob Acres. And then
there is Sir Lucius. Originally, the unrevised text was
quite explicit, for in that text Sir Lucius cries out at one
point, ". . . we must fight, for it appears that we are all
rivals."

In other respects, the two plays so close in time and
purpose, are not dissimilar. As noted, there are in both
two young couples overcoming the obstacles to true
love; there is in each play the country oaf who contri-
butes to the action as well as to the satirical humor; also
there is in each the elderly Aunt or guardian. In both
plays she is ridiculously pretentious: in Goldsmith's
comedy her pretention is to high fashion and elegant
style; in Sheridan's to copiously erudite expression and
amorous intrigue. In both works, the elderly lady's pre-
tentions are mocked at in a special scene: Old Mrs. Hardcastle by the sophisticated Hastings (Act II of *She Stoops
to Conquer*), and Mrs. Malaprop by Captain Absolute
(Act III, Scene 3 of *The Rivals*). Both elderly ladies
wield economic power to such a degree that their nieces
must not marry without their consent. In both there is
the comedy of the intercepted letter, in which the elderly
guardian reads unflattering comments on herself: Old
Mrs. Hardcastle reads, "as the hag (ay, the hag) your
mother" and Mrs. Malaprop reads of herself, "the old
weather-beaten she-dragon . . . the old harridan's consent." Considering the resemblances, it was fitting that a
considerable portion of the cast who acted in *The Rivals*
should have appeared previously in *She Stoops to Conquer*: Mr. Shuter doing both Old Mr. Hardcastle and

Sir Anthony; Mr. Quick portraying the country oafs,
Lumpkin and Acres; Mrs. Bulkley acting Kate Hardcastle
and Julia Melville; and Mrs. Green assuming the roles of
the absurd ladies, Old Mrs. Hardcastle and Mrs. Malaprop. Since Sheridan was disposed to fit character to
actor, the cast may account for some similarities in
conception.

Such parallels are typical of Sheridan's ability to
breathe new life into previously used materials, and there
are many other echoes in *The Rivals* of earlier plays and
characters. For instance, Sir Anthony is clearly modelled
on the brusque, heavy father of Congreve's *Love for
Love,* Sir Sampson Legend; Mrs. Malaprop, in her speci-
fic character of misuser of words has as her prototype
Lady Wishfort of Congreve's *The Way of the World.* A
more immediate model was Mrs. Tryfort of the *Journey
to Bath* by Sheridan's mother, wherein we find *contagion,
progeny,* and *punctuality* misused as in *The Rivals.*
Sheridan's borrowing hand was not more reluctant in
literary matters than it was in financial: almost the en-
tirety of David's homely realism concerning death and
honor (Act IV, Scene 1) is a literal paraphrase of the
more cynical meditations of Shakespeare's Falstaff in
Henry IV, Part I, and Julia Melville's finest line, in
which she describes herself to Faulkland as one whose
love was such that she "would have followed you in
beggary through the world" (Act V, Scene 1) recalls to
us Juliet's equally passionate promise, "And all my fortunes at thy foot I'll lay, and follow thee my lord throughout the world." Now and then a good line of old Sir
Anthony reminds us of Sir Geoffrey Cimberton of
Steele's *Conscious Lovers*: when Captain Absolute pro-
fesses his astonishment at his father's offering him a fortune "saddled with a wife," the bellowing father replies,
"Odds life, sir! if you have the estate you must take it
with the live stock on it as it stands." Cimberton, in
Steele's play, in a comparable situation, remarks, "You
know . . . the better sort of people . . . treat by their
lawyers of weddings, and the women in the bargain, like

the mansion house in the . . . estate, is thrown in, and
what that is, whether good or bad, is not at all considered."

In this last instance, Sheridan's more pointed and more
ingenious analogy clearly improves on the original. And
in most instances of his borrowing, Sheridan exhibits his
peculiar grace—that of lavishness: he gets his effects by
elaborating as fully as possible on his given situation or
character. In the case of Mrs. Malaprop's misuse of
language, her predecessors like Lady Wishfort or Mrs.
Tryfort essay a few sparse malapropisms; but with Mrs.
Malaprop the English language sprawls and tumbles bril-
liantly about the stage in a carnival of dazzling, acrobatic
misusage. Or if Faulkland reminds us of Hamlet in that
his mind is "sicklied o'er with the pale cast of thought,"
he distinctly out-Hamlets Hamlet: in his querulous,
fretful, microscopic analysis of motive, his perverse re-
versals of mood, he is a quivering and ludicrous specimen of amatory hypochondria. In point of jealousy,
Faulkland is reminiscent of Shakespeare's Othello. But
Othello's raging jealousy is plausible only as the product
of the skill of a superb *agent provocateur,* whereas Faulkland can from a single swallow of incident conjure up
the hottest summer of lechery: a single vicious mind in
an entire assembly will spread a contagion, "their quivering, warm-breathed sighs impregnate the very air — the
atmosphere becomes electrical to love, and each amorous
spark darts through every link of the chain!" In his gay
and dazzling elaboration of character and situation, Sheridan seems to feel about comedy what in his subsequent
life he felt about the bottle, the boudoir, the parliamentary debate, about debts — only in glorious redundance
is there sufficiency.

It is also obvious that Sheridan borrowed only when
such borrowings reflected his own interests or contrib-
uted to his own purposes. For much of the inspiration of
The Rivals appears to have been autobiographical. Sir
Lucius may well have been suggested by the irascible and
flamboyant Captain Mathews who twice involved Sheri-

dan in a duel. Mathews was a man who, like Sir Lucius, thought, "Can a man commit a more heinous offense against another than to fall in love with the same woman?" The woman in real life was, of course, Elizabeth Linley who married Sheridan. The youthful Sheridan had been involved in a romantic elopement only to be required to marry again more formally and prosaically at home. The whole exciting episode may be projected into the *Rivals* in a mood of good-natured gaiety, and Elizabeth Linley (whose name is not phonetically dissimilar to Lydia Languish) may have felt something analogous to Lydia's lament about having "to go simpering up to the altar . . . to be cried three times in a country church, and have an unmannerly fat clerk ask the consent of every butcher in the parish . . ."

But if these elements of the play were suggested by Sheridan's own experiences, the principal purpose of the *Rivals* is clearly to continue the attack of Goldsmith's *She Stoops to Conquer* on the entire eighteenth century tradition of sentimental comedies. The sentimental comedy had originated in a revulsion against the Restoration comedies of Etherege, Dryden, Wycherly, and Congreve, which had presented a world of self-indulgent moral egotism, of cheating, wayward wives and double-dealing friends, of chilling *sang-froid* and cynical sex-intrigue, of predatory gallantry and passionless passion, of finicking fops and cuckolding courtiers. In a horrified reaction against plays that were cynical, sensual, and astringent, the new sentimental comedy had become moral, edifying, and didactic, employing characters who uttered lofty sentiments and whose sensibilities were delicately refined to appreciate goodness of heart and to be horrified at crassness of any sort. In poking fun at the sentimental tradition, Sheridan's play employs two couples, each of which embodies sense and sensibility in superficial conflict despite fundamental sex-attraction. The sense of Captain Absolute is in conflict with the sensibility of Lydia Languish. As if to be fair to both sexes, Sheridan presents a secondary couple in which the sense of Julia is in con-

trast to the sensibility of Faulkland. The device of using
two couples was very effective dramatically because it
permitted the playwright to keep the contrast before the
audience's eyes not only in dialogues between the lovers
but also in conversations between the two young men
and between the two young women.

The name of Languish itself humorously recalls the
sentimental tradition of heroines full of doleful languish-
ing rather than sprightly wit. Lydia's determination to
refuse the advances of a wealthy suitor is a parody of
Leigh's *Kensington Gardens,* a sturdy specimen of sentimental comedy, in which the heroine hides her wealth in
order to ensure her being loved solely for herself, a type
of heroine which the sentimental tradition treated with
serious deference. Faulkland embodies the sentimental
tradition's morbid preoccupation with "purity" of affection; Lydia represents a similar school-girlish addiction
to "purity" of courtship and romance.

As the representative of sense, on the other hand, Captain Absolute shows a healthy respect for the economic
basis of romance, a respect which he expresses in his
parody of swooning sentiment: "Proud of calamity, we
will enjoy the wreck of wealth; while the surrounding
gloom of adversity shall make the flame of our pure love
show doubly bright . . . If she holds out now, the devil
is in it!" It should be here noted that the eighteenth century valuation placed upon property and money should
not be regarded *ipso facto* as "materialism." We may
forget too easily that theirs was a frozen economy: money
and power flowed through the rigidly preserved channels
of hereditary succession and influence. There was nothing of our fluid economy where, as it is said, you can "go
out and get it." Hence the steps leading to the marriage
altar were often the stepping stones to affluence. One
who disdained the blending of economic with sacramen-
tal graces was regarded as weak-witted. Captain Absolute
is the spirit of sense, not only in regard to his own views
of Lydia's vagaries, but likewise of Faulkland's. The Captain's general attitude towards Faulkland is one of good-

natured, satiric tolerance. The motive-scrutinizing per-
versity of Faulkland's nature is as much a parody of the
introverted, melancholy lover as Lydia's is that of the
dream-bound reader of current romances. Her story-book
whimsicality even leads her to invent a quarrel with
"Ensign Beverly" by means of writing a letter to herself.
As an imaginative stratagem it looks forward to Cecily
Cardew (of Wilde's *Importance of Being Earnest*) who
in her diary makes and breaks engagements with a fiancé
who has not yet been introduced to her.

The real index to Lydia's sensibility is the list of book-
titles given in Act I, Scene 2, the spoils of the "sub-
versive" circulating library. All of the items, whether
new publications, new translations from the wicked
French, or new editions were well known to Sheridan's
audience. *The Innocent Adultery,* for example, from the
French of Paul Scarron, had been reviewed by a popular
magazine as a "thoroughly indecent romance." On the
other hand, works such as *The Tears of Sensibility,* from
the French of M. d'Arnaud, had been applauded as being
"a miracle of sentiment and delicacy," and as drawing
human nature "warmly but chastely." *The Fatal Connexion* by "Mrs. Fogarty" received diverse notices: *The
Monthly Review* of August, 1773 applauded the author
as one "begotten, born, nursed, and educated in a circulating library" and as one who "sucked in the spirit of
romance with her mother's milk," whereas the *London
Magazine* of the same period remarked tartly, "Romantic nonsense, as usual." *The Mistakes of the Heart* by Mr.
Treyssac de Vergy was, like some of the others, a novel
in the manner of Richardson and Rousseau, simulating
the tremulous, over-wrought nervous emotion of the
former and the soaring passion of the latter. It was cast
in the epistolary form, the narrative being drawn out
through a series of intimate letters, a form valued by the
eighteenth century as emotional "realism," as giving the
"close-up." *The Town and Country Magazine* viewed
this work ambiguously, remarking that "we might recom-
mend it to the ladies if there were not some scenes too

luxuriant for the eye of delicacy." Practically all of the
works cited stimulated a taste for impossible erotic ad-
venture, a yearning for exotic amorous experience sup-
ported by an extravagant code of conduct. Lydia is as
much a satire on the sentimental novel of Sheridan's time
as of the sentimental heroine of drama.

One of the peculiarities of the play is that the secondary plot, involving the trial and ordeal of the relatively
sensible Julia Melville along with the absurdity of Faulkland, is written in two different keys; in a major key
making clear the obsessive absurdity of the latter, and in
a minor key sympathetically developing the pathos of
Julia's situation, and presenting her as a type of the
loyal, tenderly affectionate, nobly suffering heroine. This
latter aspect of her character is, of course, a reversion
to the sentimental drama which Sheridan's play is presumably ridiculing, for it leads to that kind of comedy
which Steele in his Preface to *The Conscious Lovers* said
taught the audience "to think and feel, not merely laugh
and applaud." For when Julia's all-enduring patience
finally subdues and calms Faulkland's quivering sensibility, we are confronted with — from her standpoint —
if not the Wordsworthian sadness too deep for tears, at
least Steele's "joy too exquisite for laughter." And this
kind of happiness and tender reconciliation after heart-
burning misunderstanding is the stuff of sentimental
drama. Moreover, Julia's speeches are heavily studded
with "sentiments" and are often as ornate in form as they
are solemn in content. Curiously, even the sentimental
Lydia seems refreshing in contrast to the sober Julia,
especially when she dismisses as of no emotional significance Faulkland's reported saving of Julia from drowning. Lydia quips, "Obligation! why a water spaniel
would have done as much! — Well, I should never think
of giving my heart to a man because he could swim!"
Certainly the closing speech of the play is a fine example
of the stiffly embroidered sentimental maxim, studded
with metaphors of *pencils, colors, crowns, garlands,
thorns, flowers,* and *dropping leaves* — all choked up into

one congested sentiment, not illuminated but obscured by its figurative setting.

For this split in Sheridan's comic vision, we are indebted — in part, perhaps — to his audience and the critics. For critics of the play differed sharply and strongly on the Julia-Faulkland scenes. For example, the *Morning Chronicle* of January 18, 1775 said, ". . . some of the scenes were last night insufferably tedious . . . the characters of Faulkland and Julia are even beyond the pitch of *sentimental* comedy, and may not be improperly styled, *metaphysical . . .*" *Town and Country Magazine* asserted of the characters: ". . . those of Faulkland and Miss Melville are the most *outré* sentimental ones that ever appeared upon the stage." On the other hand, in the same edition of the *Morning Chronicle,* in a letter modestly signed "One of the Pit," we learn: "Faulkland is a great proof of heart-felt delicacy; he is a beautiful exotic, and tho' not found in every garden, we cannot deny it may in some; the exquisite refinement in his disposition, opposed to the noble simplicity, tenderness, and candor of Julia's, gives rise to some of the most affecting sentimental scenes I ever remember to have met with. The general applause of the audience was proof enough of the merit of these scenes." Sheridan was a man sensitive to theatrical effect, and however humorless the Pit-critic, he was certainly literate, and Sherry would not have overlooked "the general applause." Again, the editorial opinion of the *London Review* for February, 1775 affirmed, "The characters of Faulkland and Julia display an admirable turn for nice observation on the workings of the human heart; in which respect they are perhaps inferior to nothing ever exhibited on the English stage."

With Sheridan's sense of audience, it is not remarkable that in revising the play in the hopes of making it acceptable to the town he should have permitted no marked abridgment of the Faulkland-Julia scenes. Indeed, the curtain speech of Julia just alluded to is part of the embroidery added in a revision that aimed primarily at greatly compressing an over-long play. There is, however, one notable cut in a Faulkland speech. Perhaps the attitude of his audience towards the "exquisite refinement" of Faulkland prompted Sheridan to suppress the speech to which Julia replies, "I know not whither your insinuations would tend: — but as they seem pressing to insult me . . ." The original speech of Faulkland just before these lines was: "If Marriage were but a Creature of Civil Prudence, — and we — which Heaven Knows, I would not wish — sincerely thought it to be no more, — would you forego all Pleasures of Society, all Respect, Fashion, and Customary Amusements, to smile upon our Free Faith, and Solitary Love?" In spite of the "which Heaven knows, I would not wish," Faulkland appears to be broaching something like Free Love or Companionate Marriage. Hence the bridling attitude of Julia, who leaves in indignation. Curiously with this deletion, it is difficult to see why Julia in the present purified text feels especially offended; the point at which she now experiences her flash of irritation does not seem any more trying than any other manifestation of Faulkland's worries. But on the hypothesis that Faulkland was inviting Julia to be his mistress rather than his lawful wedded wife, her attitude is comprehensible.

Sheridan here cut a piece from the garment without bothering to stitch the edges together again. This kind of deletion suggests that he was trying to live up to the "exquisite refinement" evaluation of Faulkland. And in a revision urgently aimed at shortening, not extending, he adds to Julia's already heart-full speeches such artificially elaborated lines as "Then on the bosom of your wedded Julia, you may lull your keen regret to slumbering; while virtuous love, with a cherub's hand, shall smoothe the brow of upbraiding thought, and pluck the thorn from compunction." It seems fairly clear that in revising his text Sheridan the ambitious playwright exacted concessions from Sheridan the wit and satirist. The result is a comedy-creature which moves irregularly and unevenly on all fours; one couple who are to provoke our mirth, another who are to be taken seriously.

Actually, we do not have the manuscript of *The Rivals* as it was originally produced; what we do have, the Larpent Ms., is a copy of the original, a copy to be sent to the Lord Chamberlain, official licenser of plays. The existing Ms. is probably close to the original, if not an exact duplication. A critic for *The Monthly Miscellany* for February of 1775 summarizes the original perform-ance (and in the narration of incident he agrees with the Larpent Ms.) as follows:

The Rivals, Tuesday, Jan. 17. At the *first* performance of this play . . . either from the badness of the piece itself, the negligence of the performers, or the wrong casting of the parts, it met with a very indifferent reception; but the author has since retouched it, and on its *second* appearance, Jan. 28, it met with great applause . . .

The fable stood thus: Miss Lydia Languish, a young lady of £30,000 fortune, is addressed by Captain Absolute, the son of Sir Anthony Absolute, under the fictitious title of Ensign Beverley. Two-thirds of her fortune, however, are settled upon another branch of (the) family, if she marries without the consent of her aunt Malaprop; which causes no small hesitation on the part of the Captain . . .

In this situation the lovers are found at Bath, where Sir Anthony unexpectedly arrives . . . surprised to find his son there; however, he presently informs the Captain that he has a wife in his eye for him, and insists on his assent, with-out so much as seeing the lady. This the Captain positively refuses . . . and his father leaves with threats to disinherit him. The Captain, soon discovering that the choice . . . was no other than that he had pitched on for himself, pleads his penitence . . . promises to obey him, be the lady whom or what she may.

In consequence [he] is introduced by Sir Anthony to Mrs. Malaprop as Captain Absolute . . . to be presented to her niece as her admirer.

The old lady . . . informs him of a young beggarly Ensign to whom Lydia was a little partial . . . no great danger now, as she had discovered the plot by a letter she had inter-

cepted, which she begs him to read, in which the old lady
is finely abused, with respect to her figure and affectation of
using hard words. Lydia being introduced . . . is much astonished at finding her Beverley is Captain Absolute; he tells
her, however, that he assumed the name . . . only to gain
admission to her . . . however, on his father's entrance the
deceit is discovered, and . . . Lydia's hopes of an elopement
being all cut off, she treats the idea of the union by the
consent of their parents with great indifference, and they
part with no very favourable impression of each other.

Mr. Acres arrives about this time at Bath, on a visit of
courtship to this same lady, but he is refused admittance. He
is waited upon by Sir Lucius O'Trigger, to whom he relates
his grievances. Sir Lucius immediately recommends him to
call the favourite lover to an account, to which Acres con-
sents, by writing a challenge, which, in order to prevent a
prosecution, he signs with the name of Colin, and sends it
to the lover of Miss Languish . . . insisting on his meeting
him in King's-mead.

Sir Lucius himself, through the artifice of Lucy, Lydia's
maid, has been made to believe that her mistress was dying
for love of him, from a letter she carried to him, written by
the old aunt, who . . . has a predilection for this gigantic
fortune-hunter.

In consequence of his supposed pretensions to Lydia, he
designedly quarrels with the Captain, whom he meets on the
Parade, supposing him his rival; and insists upon his giving
him satisfaction in King's-mead, where he has a little affair
of the same nature upon his hands.

David, Acres' servant . . . arrives with his master's challenge, and supposing Sir Lucius to be the rival, delivers it to
him, who, mistaking it, as it is only subscribed Colin, for a
note from the Captain, posts away to the field.

By the time the combatants are supposed to have arrived
at their ground, David alarms the whole town, while Mrs.
Malaprop, Lydia, Sir Anthony, Mr. Faulkland, and Julia
Melville with constables, &c., soon after arrive, and prevent
the fatal effects of a duel by a general eclairisement, which
terminates the comedy by the old aunt's giving her hand to
Sir Lucius, and the marriage of Captain Absolute with Miss
Languish.

An episode, containing a number of disputes between Miss

Julia and Faulkland, who is ever doubtful of the affection of his mistress . . . puts her constancy to the severest trials, makes a very agreeable addition to the principal story . . .

Its present state is widely different from that in which it appeared on the first night's representation. Sir Lucius O'Trigger, being retouched, has now the appearance of a character; and his assigning Beverley's reflection on his country, as the grounds for his desire to quarrel with him, is a reasonable pretence, and wipes off the former stigma undeservedly thrown on the sister kingdom. An alteration of a principal incident gave a very favourable turn to the fable and the whole piece; viz. that when young Acres now delivers his challenge to his friend Absolute, begging him to carry it to his rival Beverley, not knowing the two characters composed but one man; its being at first given to Sir Lucius, the person who indited it, was highly inconsistent. The performers were now very attentive to their duty.

This summary touches upon most issues pertinent to the history of the play. One of the main ingredients of the "badness of the piece" was its inordinate length in the original form. One contemporary observes that it was "a full hour longer than any piece on the stage." Another reviewer affirmed that the play lasted four hours, indicating the almost Shavian presumption of the young writer. A play time-table of 1767 reports that the two longest plays then in the tradition were Jonson's *Volpone* (two and a half hours) and Gay's *Beggar's Opera* (three hours). The facts agree. Also included in the "badness" was the figure of Sir Lucius, mentioned toward the end of the summary.

The changes in the text involved not only alteration of the character of Sir Lucius and incidents referring to him, but considerable suppression and revision of dialogue. Although the press inveighed against the atrocious instances of Sheridan's pontifical heaviness, it made no mention of his occasional employment of obvious *double entendre* and salacious overtone. In fact, Sheridan carefully expunged both types of offense. He also excised such types of pun as that in which he had allowed Fag to speak of Ovid's *Metamorphoses* as Ovid's "Meat-for-

horses," and to call Jupiter "Juniper." As one reviewer
observed, these were "contemptible" efforts at wit "even
for a postillion." The young Sheridan readily substituted
critical sense for loose exuberance and rid his text of
most such excrescences. He also established a monopoly
of misusage in favor of Mrs. Malaprop, thus establishing
her as the queen of solecism, who deranges epitaphs so
nicely that she was not rivalled until Finnegan was awak-
ened by Joyce. Some of her less successful efforts were
suppressed; some were improved: "vermillion" tongue
was changed to "oracular" tongue, for example. Some
fairly amusing instances were quietly dropped, such as
the conclusion of a letter to Sir Lucius from Delia: "As
my motive is interested, you may be assured my love
shall never be miscellaneous . . . Yours, while meretricious, . . ." Other changes were aimed at purification,
such as the change of "perforate my Mystery" to "dis-
solve my Mystery."

A large number of alterations were evidently suggested by criteria of "refinement" and "gentility." The
original Sir Anthony, for example, was slightly touched
with the goatish and satyr-like temper of Restoration
fathers; he was originally closer to his prototype Sir Sam-
son Legend of Congreve's *Love for Love,* already mentioned. In speaking of the consequences of circulating
libraries, he referred to "our London nunneries" as their
beneficiaries and went on to speak of their connection
with a special kind of "Recruiting Officer." He meant
"brothels" and "pimps." In the original version he raged
against his son when the latter facetiously pretended to
complete indifference to female charm and to be solici-
tous only of conformity to his father's will: "So lifeless a
clod as you should not dare to approach the Arms of
glowing Beauty — to lie like a Cucumber, on a hot bed."
And when Mrs. Malaprop and Sir Anthony break in upon
Lydia and Captain Absolute, they misunderstand Lydia's
tears, actually the tears of the romantic school-girl disappointed at learning that there is to be not an elopement but only a formal marriage. Both Mrs. Malaprop

and Sir Anthony suspect that Captain Absolute has been prematurely and aggressively exploring nuptial mysteries; most of the following (except for the addition of one "ha!") was cut down in the revised version to read, ". . . you have been too lively, Jack." The original read:

MRS. MALAPROP: . . . why, sure, Captain, you ha'n't been attempting — O Lud! I shall swoon at the Thought.

SIR ANTHONY: Ha! ha! ha! ha! ha! . . . why you confounded young Rogue, couldn't you wait for the Parson — You must be in such a damn'd hurry?

CAPTAIN ABSOLUTE: Nay, Sir, upon my word —

SIR ANTHONY: . . . you have been rude . . . I know it. Ah! Mrs. Malaprop, these young Soldiers must never be trusted with a pretty Girl, Tete a Tete — Like Children, they will be picking at the Dish, before Mama has pinn'd the Napkin.

MRS. MALAPROP: O Lud, Sir Anthony, you make me blush so!

This sort of "roguish" dialogue had descended from the Restoration stage: Sir Sampson Legend had said of his son Ben, "Ben's a brisk boy: He has got her into a Corner, Father's own son, faith, he'll touzle her, and mouzle her! The Rogue's sharp set, coming from Sea; if he should not stay for saying Grace . . . but fall to without the help of a Parson, ha? . . . *a chip of the old Block.*" *Block* is perhaps the right word. This somewhat weary waggishness passed in mid-century through Fielding's *Tom Jones* on the way to Sheridan: of the erring Nancy Miller, Partridge had said, "In short, Miss Nancy hath had a mind to be as wise as her mother; that's all, she was a little hungry, it seems, and so sat down to dinner before grace was said; and so there is a child coming for the Foundling Hospital."

When Lockhart reviewed the *Memoirs* of Sheridan for the *Quarterly Review* for March of 1828, he commented on the purity of Sheridan's taste and the chasteness of his dialogue. With Sheridan, it had been a matter of literary discipline, not natural feeling, as an inspection of his original text reveals. By 1826, the effects of the Evangelical revival were being fully felt, as Lockhart's

consciousness of this aspect of Sheridan's work reflects.
But Sheridan, moving in a circle quite outside that of the
Evangelicals, was evidently moved by considerations of
gentility and high feeling, rather than of morality.

The reviews almost unanimously denounced the actors
of the original performance for not having learned their
parts, so much so that more than half the play on the
opening night appears to have been recited by the promp-
ter. By our modern standards of meticulous production,
the conditions described seem incredible. Besides poor
preparation there was poor casting: Mr. Shuter played
Sir Anthony, and Mr. Woodward, Captain Absolute —
the former at forty-seven years of age being "father" to
Mr. Woodward who was sixty-one, a paternity too precocious for Sheridan's audience to relish. A greater piece
of miscasting seems to have been that of Mr. Lee as Sir
Lucius (he was succeeded by the eminently satisfactory
Laurence Clinch in the second version); Lee was denounced equally by audience and critics. Whether "so
villainous a portrait of any Irish gentleman" was to be
attributed mainly to Lee's performance or Sheridan's
text has been and is argued; apparently it was an involun-
tary collaboration. A contemporary records Lee's per-
plexity on this point. Hit in the last act on the head with
an apple, Lee stepped forward and demanded in a loud
rich brogue, "By the powers, is it personal? — is it me,
or the matter?" Whichever it was, the audience felt that
the part was a savage caricature of the Irish gentleman.
Presumably it was at least in part Sheridan's fault, for
his original text presented a Sir Lucius who was unsympathetic. He was obvious, if not coarse; he was occasionally
silly; and he was also a transparent marital adventurer,
for although young and personable, he married old Mrs.
Malaprop at the end of the play.

But Lee's acting was evidently preposterous. *The
Morning Chronicle* of January 20, 1775 reported him as
speaking in a "horrid medley of discordant brogues," a
further installment of the criticism it had made two days
earlier in referring to him as "gabbling in an uncouth

dialect, neither Welsh, English, nor Irish." A vain man, enamoured of his successful performances of Iago, Lear, and Hamlet, Lee found the role beneath him and left it lower still. It is notable that in our present version Sir Lucius is neither an adventurer nor a fool. Besides suppressions, Sheridan carefully introduced such lines as those given to Lucy, who speaking of Sir Lucius says, ". . . he had too much pride and delicacy to sacrifice the feelings of a gentleman to the necessities of his fortune." This reversal of the original character evidently averted an international crisis at the time. *The Morning Chronicle* of January 30, 1775 commented on the alterations characteristically: "We heartily wish it was a general custom for authors to withdraw their pieces after a first performance, in order to . . . generally amend the play . . . his comedy is much altered for the better . . . and all the performers . . . better acquainted with their several parts . . . It comes within a reasonable compass as to the time taken up in the representation . . . and although we cannot pronounce it, with all its amendments, a comic chef-d'oeuvre, it certainly encourages us to hope for a very capital play from the same writer at a future season." The *School for Scandal* quite fulfilled this oblique prophecy.

But the earlier play still remains one of the outstanding comedies of the eighteenth century and one of the most memorable of English comedies. It may lay claim to uniqueness as the comedy of the twisted countenance: the muse expresses on one side of her face the solemnity of tender solicitude; on the other, the wrinkles of boisterous laughter; it is a special eighteenth century Sheridanblend of grave and gay. The true spirit of comedy dances on a tight-rope. In the comedy of manners tradition, the comic spirit is ideally neither so superior to its materials as to embody itself in a satiric expression nor so involved as to provoke sympathy. Its ideal position is rational detachment and objectivity. But such a position is more intellectual than mirthful. Hence the comic spirit is always in danger of falling on one side of the rope to the ground of farce or satire; on the other, into sentiment. Sheridan, always a creature of irrepressible exuberance (himself half-satiric, half-sentimental), dances on both sides of the rope — and occasionally on it.

On the satiric-farcical side, Sheridan satirizes two traditions: one in literature, one in life. He makes fun of duelling, the last flickering expression of the tradition of chivalry; he mocks the pseudo-chivalrous eighteenth century novel of sentiment, a completely unreal mode of viewing life, an attitude nourished by a literature of precious sensibility, lacking all elements of reality. Hence the Lydia Languish-Captain Absolute plot makes game of the bookish romance of clandestine correspondence, vigilant intercepting aunts, servant-intermediaries (half-sympathetic, half-mercenary), its extravagant yearnings for a romantic elopement leading to the water of poverty and disinheritance, but somehow to be miraculously transformed at the wedding repast into wine. *The Rivals* is a laughing obituary of this now-incredible literary vogue. The custom of duelling, not to vanish until well into the next century, is laughed at as the obsession of country lumpkins turned swordsmen and amiable monomaniacs like Sir Lucius who can find cause for a quarrel of honor in the barking of a neighbor's dog.

In addition is the sentimental comedy of the too patient, too true, too blue, altogether too-too Julia, whose tender, loyal solicitude is the cold pack applied to the fevered brow of Faulkland.

Finally, we have Mrs. Malaprop, a dowager miscarriage of diction. Although her speech, the principal element of her contribution to the comedy, is without dramatic significance in respect to incident or plot, the light-hearted Sheridan cannot refrain from still another addition. He wishes to achieve an exotic composite of materials for laughter. He is determined that his spectators shall have the satisfaction of a plenary indulgence in the temple of mirth.

THE STAGING

Physically, the eighteenth century theatre was very much like that of our own day; it was, in fact the beginning of the modern theatre. The Renaissance and baroque drama of the preceding sixteenth and seventeenth centuries had possessed two quite different traditions. First, there were the popular plays presented commercially in theatres often improvised from inn-yards and indoor tennis courts. Here, as far as production was concerned, the rule of economy prevailed and there was a minimum of scenery. The audience, standing in the "pit" or seated in the encircling galleries, surrounded the actors, who performed mainly on an apron platform that projected well out from the stage proper. But if the physical characteristics of the popular theatre were meager, the intellectual and psychological ones were not. The intricacy of Renaissance plots is famous, as is the richness and variety of metaphor in the actors' lines.

The second tradition which developed during the years preceding the eighteenth century was that of the court gala, especially gotten up to celebrate the marriage or coronation of some member of the ruling family. Here, elaborate scenery and costumes were primary attractions, and no expense was spared. Fantastic palaces, at the wink of an eye, were changed into gushing fountains, rocky eyries, or distant battlefields. The actors in these masques (as they were called) were sometimes professional, but often members of the court; even kings and queens took part. Needless to say, no great histrionic demands were made upon the participants. Indeed, in a masque, the plot was perhaps the least significant consideration.

In the eighteenth century these two traditions united into one which still persists today. From the popular theatres of Shakespeare and Molière came the notion of a highly plotted narrative demanding considerable acting ability; and from the court masque came the tradition of quickly changing painted scenery.

In England, with the eventual relaxation of the 1737 law which governed the licensing of public performances, the popular theatre could operate more freely. Theatregoing became a fashionable recreation, and producers in the so-called "illegitimate" houses were able to realize a profit even in their smaller auditoriums. In London there were buildings such as the Opera House in Haymarket boasting enormous stages which could accommodate the full machinery for descending clouds and rushing rivers — effects still called for in Italian operas. But most eighteenth century theatres were more modest in their dimensions; often their stages were tiny by modern standards. Sometimes there was barely room for the actors.

Whether the stage was large or small, the scenic equipment was something like this. On either side of the stage was a set of wooden frames, which could run on and off stage in grooves in the floor, suspended overhead on a wheel and track system such as we sometimes see used for sliding barn doors. These wooden frames were covered with canvas and hid the offstage portions of the theatre. They were called "wings." Much larger frames, called "flats," operated in the same way but met in the center to provide the back wall of the set. Across the top of each set of wings was a canvas strip called a "border" which extended across the stage and served as masking to hide the upper part of the stage house from the audience. All these scenic elements were painted to represent some indoor or outdoor scene.

When the locale of the play had to be changed, the wings and flats could be drawn offstage in their grooves, revealing another set of flats and wings with a different scene painted on them. All details of a given scene were painted on the flats, even furniture and properties, except for those objects which the actors actually used. Eighteenth century actors rarely sat down so there was not apt to be much furniture about.

The stage opening, or proscenium arch, was often elaborately decorated, and usually boxes for the spectators were housed in it. From these box seats you could easily look down on the apron, but you could not see the stage proper without craning your neck. This indicates that the apron was where the actors spent most of their time, the area behind being reserved mainly for scenery. Thus the eighteenth century stage-setting was more of a *backing*

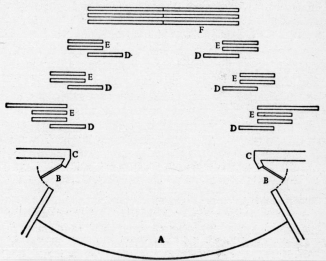

Diagram of a typical late eighteenth-century stage

A is the apron upon which most of the action took place; B, the proscenium doors; C, the proscenium opening behind which the curtain hung. The onstage wings are marked D, and those off-stage, awaiting their turn to be used, are marked E. Behind the first set of wings are a pair of shutters which can close the stage completely off for scenes in hallways and other constricted quarters. The back shutters are marked F.

for the actor, in contrast to the modern set, which *encloses* him. On each side of the proscenium arch was a door which led from the offstage area to the apron. Actors made their entrances and exits through these doors or through the spaces between the wings.

The audience not only occupied the normal orchestra seats, but also several tiers of boxes which curved around the inside of the auditorium like giant horse-shoes with their open ends toward the stage. Many of the older theatres in this country, such as the Metropolitan Opera House in New York (1882) still retain this horse-shoe arrangement for box seats and balconies. This form may have had its origin in the converted inn-yards where popular theatre was staged in the sixteenth and seventeenth centuries.

This picture of a typical eighteenth century theatre, as we remarked at the beginning, reminds us of a modern theatre, especially compared to what had gone before. But if our theatres have changed only a little and if we still occasionally use wing and border sets, there are important differences between our method of staging a play and the traditional method of the eighteenth century. One of these differences involves a whole new attitude towards change of scenery. In the eighteenth century theatre, the curtain was not closed at the end of a scene. Instead, a uniformed factotum came out after the actors had left and removed or rearranged all the properties for the next scene. Then the wings and shutters slid back, and the borders were raised *a vista* (in sight of the audience) by unseen hands backstage, revealing the new set in the manner described above. These *a vista* changes were part of the fun of going to the theatre, and audiences might well have felt cheated if the curtain had hidden them. As a matter of fact, this popular relic of baroque theatre practice did not disappear until the last century.

While the modern theatre-goer, schooled in the complete representationalism of Hollywood and Broadway, may object that these painted scenes must rarely have been very convincing, let him remember that the revealing brilliance of modern electric lighting did not yet exist. Eighteenth century scenery was lighted only by the flickering of myriads of candles. Chandeliers were hung backstage between the wings and borders, and also out in the auditorium. These auditorium lights, by the way, were *not* extinguished during performances.

Another important difference between eighteenth century practice and our own lies in the sphere of costume. In the eighteenth century no distinction was made between "modern dress" and "period" productions. An actor, whether he played Hamlet or an eighteenth century gentleman, wore either everyday dress or a kind of special "actor's costume" such as we see in Watteau's paintings of Italian comedians. One actress of the period, it is recorded, did give a Roman matron the classic toga she deserved, but insisted on wearing it over a hoopskirt!

This everyday eighteenth century dress was quite elaborate, however. Men wore black or white silk stockings and pumps decorated with fancy buckles. Their trousers consisted of tight breeches buckled just below the knee. They also wore capacious waistcoats and jackets with skirts or tails in back which descended to the knees. Lace bands were worn at the neck and lace cuffs at the wrists. The three-cornered hat with cockade or feather topped off the ensemble. The men of the eighteenth century had no compunctions about wearing bright and highly decorated materials, brocaded or printed in strong and colorful patterns. The tradition of black, brown, and gray which now dominates men's everyday dress did not set in until the nineteenth century.

Women wore pumps, too, and long stiff skirts and bodices as colorful as the men's suits. Skirts were almost always worn over hoops, and were often split up the center to reveal a contrasting underskirt. Sometimes panniers (wicker or wire frames which expanded the apparent width of the hips) were worn instead of hoopskirts. Over these the skirts were often draped in festoons which could end in short trains. Women's bodices were cut to a sharp point at the waist and in a very low curved or square neckline. Sleeves were elbow length, terminating in lace ruffles. White powdered wigs, very high, were worn by all fashionable women for dress occasions, often in combination with plumes.

The elegant everyday dress, the *a vista* scene change (which probably groaned and creaked enormously), the lighted auditorium, and above all the artificial quality of the painted wings and flats — these things are to be kept in mind when we try to reconstruct the production of eighteenth century plays. Remember, too, that the play was not a classic when it first appeared. Audiences did not listen in worshipful silence. Perhaps they found themselves more amusing than the play: at any rate they were apt to chatter during many of the scenes, and only during the most important speeches by favorite actors and actresses was there absolute silence. During these scenes the fans punctuated every particularly good line with salvos of applause. At the end of the play the manager would come out on the apron and if he was greeted with hisses and boos he would retire in defeat, knowing that the play was a failure and that it could not be repeated. If, on the other hand, the audience's reception was reasonably enthusiastic, he would announce triumphantly: "The unparalleled success of the latest and brightest spark from the anvil of the comic muse will be repeated every evening until further notice."

For the eighteenth century audience, the theatre was more than a playhouse; it was a place where invitations were issued, assignations made, duels arranged, debutantes introduced, dowries settled, and reputations made and lost. It was a glittering spectacle of fashionable dress and histrionic partisanship.

PREFACE

A preface to a play seems generally to be considered as a kind of closet-prologue,[1] in which — if his piece has been successful — the author solicits that indulgence from the reader which he had before experienced from the audience: but as the scope and immediate object of a play is to please a mixed assembly in *representation* (whose judgment in the theatre at least is decisive), its degree of reputation is usually as determined as public, before it can be prepared for the cooler tribunal of the study. Thus any farther solicitude on the part of the writer becomes unnecessary at least, if not an intrusion: and if the piece has been condemned in the performance, I fear an address to the closet, like an appeal to posterity, is constantly regarded as the procrastination of a suit, from a consciousness of the weakness of the cause. From these considerations, the following comedy would certainly have been submitted to the reader, without any farther introduction than what it had in the representation, but that its success has probably been founded on a circumstance which the author is informed has not before attended a theatrical trial, and which consequently ought not to pass unnoticed.

I need scarcely add, that the circumstance alluded to was the withdrawing of the piece, to remove those imperfections in the first representation which were too obvious to escape reprehension, and too numerous to admit of a hasty correction. There are few writers, I believe, who, even in the fullest consciousness of error, do not wish to palliate the faults which they acknowledge; and, however trifling the performance, to second their confession of its deficiencies, by whatever plea seems least disgraceful to their ability. In the present instance, it

---

[1] Closet-drama is a play to be read; this is therefore a prologue for readers.

cannot be said to amount either to candour or modesty in me, to acknowledge an extreme inexperience and want of judgment on matters, in which, without guidance from practice, or spur from success, a young man should scarcely boast of being an adept. If it be said, that under such disadvantages no one should attempt to write a play, I must beg leave to dissent from the position, while the first point of experience that I have gained on the subject is, a knowledge of the candour and judgment with which an impartial public distinguishes between the errors of inexperience and incapacity, and the indulgence which it shows even to a disposition to remedy the defects of either.

It were unnecessary to enter into any farther extenuation of what was thought exceptionable in this play, but that it has been said, that the managers should have prevented some of the defects before its appearance to the public — and in particular the uncommon length of the piece as represented the first night. It were an ill return for the most liberal and gentlemanly conduct on their side, to suffer any censure to rest where none was deserved. Hurry in writing has long been exploded as an excuse for an author; — however, in the dramatic line, it may happen, that both an author and a manager may wish to fill a chasm in the entertainment of the public with a hastiness not altogether culpable. The season was advanced when I first put the play into Mr. Harris's[2] hands: — it was at that time at least double the length of any acting comedy. I profited by his judgment and experience in the curtailing of it — till, I believe, his feeling for the vanity of a young author got the better of his desire for correctness, and he left many excrescences remaining, because he had assisted in pruning so many more. Hence, though I was not uninformed that the acts were still too long, I flattered myself that, after the first trial, I might with safer judgment proceed to remove what should appear to have been most dissatisfactory. Many other errors there were, which might in part have

---

[2] Thomas Harris was the manager of the Covent Garden Theatre.

arisen from my being by no means conversant with plays in general, either in reading or at the theatre. Yet I own that, in one respect, I did not regret my ignorance: for as my first wish in attempting a play was to avoid every appearance of plagiary, I thought I should stand a better chance of effecting this from being in a walk which I had not frequented, and where, consequently, the progress of invention was less likely to be interrupted by starts of recollection: for on subjects on which the mind has been much informed, invention is slow of exerting itself. Faded ideas float in the fancy like half-forgotten dreams; and the imagination in its fullest enjoyments becomes suspicious of its offspring, and doubts whether it has created or adopted.

With regard to some particular passages which on the first night's representation seemed generally disliked, I confess, that if I felt any emotion of surprise at the disapprobation, it was not that they were disapproved of, but that I had not before perceived that they deserved it. As some part of the attack on the piece was begun too early to pass for the sentence of *judgment,* which is ever tardy in condemning, it has been suggested to me, that much of the disapprobation must have arisen from virulence of malice, rather than severity of criticism; but as I was more apprehensive of there being just grounds to excite the latter than conscious of having deserved the former, I continue not to believe that probable, which I am sure must have been unprovoked. However, if it was so, and I could even mark the quarter from whence it came, it would be ungenerous to retort; for no passion suffers more than malice from disappointment. For my own part, I see no reason why the author of a play should not regard a first night's audience as a candid and judicious friend attending, in behalf of the public, at his last rehearsal. If he can dispense with flattery, he is sure at least of sincerity, and even though the annotation be rude, he may rely upon the justness of the comment. Considered in this light, that audience, whose *fiat* is essential to the poet's claim, whether his object be fame or profit, has surely a right to expect some deference to its opinion, from principles of politeness at least, if not from gratitude.

As for the little puny critics, who scatter their peevish strictures in private circles, and scribble at every author who has the eminence of being unconnected with them, as they are usually spleen-swoln from a vain idea of increasing their consequence, there will always be found a petulance and illiberality in their remarks, which should place them as far beneath the notice of a gentleman, as their original dulness had sunk them from the level of the most unsuccessful author.

It is not without pleasure that I catch at an opportunity of justifying myself from the charge of intending any national reflection in the character of Sir Lucius O'Trigger. If any gentlemen opposed the piece from that idea, I thank them sincerely for their opposition; and if the condemnation of this comedy (however misconceived the provocation) could have added one spark to the decaying flame of national attachment to the country supposed to be reflected on, I should have been happy in its fate; and might with truth have boasted, that it had done more real service in its failure, than the successful morality of a thousand stage-novels will ever effect.

It is usual, I believe, to thank the performers in a new play, for the exertion of their several abilities. But where (as in this instance) their merit has been so striking and uncontroverted, as to call for the warmest and truest applause from a number of judicious audiences, the poet's after-praise comes like the feeble acclamation of a child to close the shouts of a multitude. The conduct, however, of the principals in a theatre cannot be so apparent to the public. I think it therefore but justice to declare, that from this theatre (the only one I can speak of from experience) those writers who wish to try the dramatic line will meet with that candour and liberal attention, which are generally allowed to be better calculated to lead genius into excellence, than either the precepts of judgment, or the guidance of experience.

THE AUTHOR

CAST OF CHARACTERS

in the order of their appearance

The Prologue:

A SERJEANT-AT-LAW, a member of the upper hierarchy of the legal profession.

AN ATTORNEY, a lawyer representing the author.

The Play:

THOMAS, countrified coachman serving Sir Anthony Absolute.

FAG, dandified servant of Sir Anthony's sophisticated son.

LYDIA LANGUISH, sentimental young lady of fashion.

LUCY, scheming maid of Lydia's aging aunt.

JULIA, Lydia's wholesome cousin, ward of Sir Anthony.

LYDIA LANGUISH

MRS. MALAPROP, Lydia's fabulously fatuous aunt.

SIR ANTHONY ABSOLUTE, wealthy country gentleman of the old school.

MRS. MALAPROP

SIR ANTHONY ABSOLUTE

CAPTAIN ABSOLUTE, his handsome and dashing son.

FAULKLAND, the Captain's friend and Julia's sighing suitor.

CAPTAIN ABSOLUTE

BOB ACRES

BOB ACRES, rustic young neighbor of the Absolutes, Lydia's formal suitor.

SIR LUCIUS O'TRIGGER, flambuoyant Irish nobleman, as bold as he is bankrupt.

DAVID, Bob Acres' timid servant.

Also JULIA'S MAID, a BOY member of Captain Absolute's household staff, and miscellaneous SERVANTS.

SIR LUCIUS O'TRIGGER

SYNOPSIS OF SCENES

The entire action takes place at Bath, the fashionable watering-place of the British aristocracy. Here gathered the cream of Society to enjoy prolonged periods of idle vacationing. The British moral sense was wonderfully satisfied at this resort since it was clearly a duty of the governing class to keep fit and gain health and vigor from the medicinal waters by drinking and immersion. They were equally fortified spiritually; especially after the celebrated Beau Nash, as major-domo, had introduced both decorum and elegance by concerts, games, dances, and parties, together with the intellectual delight of conversing informally while enjoying the open air of the splendid promenades or "parades" which had been constructed. The affairs of those members of Society observed in this play occupies the space of a single day.

ACT I.
Scene 1. A Street in the City (early morning).
Scene 2. Lydia Languish's Dressing Room (shortly afterward).

ACT II.
Scene 1. Captain Absolute's Lodgings (mid-morning).
Scene 2. The North Parade (late morning).

ACT III.
Scene 1. The North Parade (early afternoon).
Scene 2. Julia's Dressing Room (a little later).
Scene 3. Mrs. Malaprop's Lodgings (shortly afterward).
Scene 4. Bob Acres' Lodgings (immediately following).

ACT IV.
Scene 1. Bob Acres' Lodgings (mid-afternoon).
Scene 2. Mrs. Malaprop's Lodgings (shortly afterward).
Scene 3. The North Parade (late afternoon).

ACT V.
Scene 1. Julia's Dressing Room (early evening).
Scene 2. The South Parade (later — a little before six).
Scene 3. King's-Mead-Fields (about six o'clock).

53

PROLOGUE
Spoken at the Opening Performance

The scene is a street in Bath. A Serjeant-at-Law enters followed by an Attorney who gives him a paper.

SERJEANT: What's here — a vile cramp hand! I cannot see
Without my spectacles.
ATTORNEY: He means his fee.
Nay, Mr. Serjeant, good sir, try again. *(Gives him money)*
SERJEANT: The scrawl improves! *(Attorney gives more)* Oh come, 'tis pretty plain.
Hey! how's this? — Dibble! — sure it cannot be!
A poet's brief! A poet and a fee!
ATTORNEY: Yea, sir! — tho' you without reward, I know,
Would gladly plead the Muse's cause —
SERJEANT: So — so!
ATTORNEY: And if the fee offends — your wrath should fall
On me —
SERJEANT: Dear Dibble, no offence at all —
ATTORNEY: Some sons of Phoebus[1] in the courts we meet,
SERJEANT: And fifty sons of Phoebus in the Fleet![2]
ATTORNEY: Nor pleads he worse, who with a decent sprig
Of bays — adorns his legal waste of wig.
SERJEANT: Full-bottomed heroes thus, on signs, unfurl
A leaf of laurel — in a grove of curl!
Yet tell your client, that, in adverse days,
This wig is warmer than a bush of bays.[3]

---

[1] Phoebus Apollo, god of poetry.
[2] A prison nearly 800 years old, destroyed in 1846. A debtor's prison as early as 1290, entirely so after 1641.
[3] Bay-berry or laurel, traditional garland or crown for literary excellence.

ATTORNEY: Do you then, sir, my client's place supply,
Profuse of robe, and prodigal of tie —
Do you, with all those blushing powers of face,
And wonted bashful hesitating grace,
Rise in the court ,and flourish on the case. *(Exit)*
    SERJEANT: For practice then suppose — this brief will
        show it —
Me, Serjeant Woodward, — counsel for the poet.
Used to the ground — I know 'tis hard to deal
With this dread court, from whence there's no appeal;
No tricking here, to blunt the edge of law,
Or, damned in equity — escape by flaw:
But judgment given — your sentence must remain;
— No writ of error lies — to Drury Lane![4]
Yet when so kind you seem — 'tis past dispute
We gain some favour, if not costs of suit.
No spleen is here! I see no hoarded fury;
— I think I never faced a milder jury!
Sad else our plight! — where frowns are transportation,
A hiss the gallows — and a groan, damnation!
But such the public candour, without fear
My client waives all right of challenge here.
No newsman from our session is dismissed,
Nor writ nor critic we scratch off the list;
His faults can never hurt another's ease,
His crime at worst — a bad attempt to please:
Thus, all respecting, he appeals to all,
And by the general voice will stand or fall.

---

[4] Location of the Theatre Royal, popularly known as the Drury
Lane theatre.

PROLOGUE

To the Revised Production, Presented on the Tenth Night.

Spoken by Julia.

Granted our cause, our suit and trial o'er,
The worthy serjeant need appear no more:
In pleasing I a different client choose,
He served the Poet — I would serve the Muse:
Like him, I'll try to merit your applause,
A female counsel in a female's cause.

      Look on this form — (pointing to COMEDY[1])
          where humor, quaint and sly,
Dimples the cheek, and points the beaming eye;
Where gay invention seems to boast its wiles
In amorous hint, and half-triumphant smiles;
While her light mask or covers satire's strokes,
Or hides the conscious blush her wit provokes.
— Look on her well — does she seem formed to teach?
Should you expect to hear this lady — preach?[2]
Is grey experience suited to her youth?
Do solemn sentiments become that mouth?
Bid her be grave, those lips should rebel prove
To every theme that slanders mirth or love.

      Yet thus adorned with every graceful art
To charm the fancy and yet reach the heart —
Must we displace her? And instead advance
The goddess of the woful countenance —
The sentimental Muse! — Her emblems view,
The Pilgrim's Progress, and a sprig of rue!
View her — too chaste to look like flesh and blood —[3]

---

[1] The images of Comedy and Tragedy appeared as carved wooden figures on either side of the proscenium arch.

[2] A reference to the solemn, didactic manner of sentimental comedy—opposed by Sheridan.

[3] A reference to the sickly, self-conscious virtue of sentimental comedy.

Primly portray'd on emblematic wood!
There fixed in usurpation should she stand,
She'll snatch the dagger from her sister's hand:
And having made her votaries weep a flood,
Good heaven! she'll end her comedies in blood —
Bid Harry Woodward break poor Dunstall's crown!
Imprison Quick — and knock Ned Shuter down;
While sad Barsanti — weeping o'er the scene —
Shall stab himself — or poison Mrs. Green.[4]
Such dire encroachments to prevent in time,
Demands the critic's voice — the poet's rhyme.
Can our light scenes add strength to holy laws?[5]
Such puny patronage but hurts the cause:
Fair virtue scorns our feeble aid to ask;
And moral truth disdains the trickster's mask.
For here their favorite stands, (pointing to TRAGEDY)
   whose brow, severe
And sad — claims youth's respect, and pity's tear;
Who — when oppressed by foes her worth creates —
Can point a poniard at the guilt she hates.

---

[4] Actors in the play.
[5] i.e., cannot a more realistic comedy of satire and laughter also provide moral insights?

ACT ONE
Scene One

A street in Bath, fashionable watering place in England. A coachman Thomas, in the employ of Sir Anthony Absolute, saunters across the stage as Fag, the dandified footman of Sir Anthony's son, approaches from the opposite direction. Thomas, somewhat older, is clearly a country man. He is devoted to his horses and to the family he has served for many years. His dark drab livery, rustic speech, and plain manner are in striking contrast to the veneer of sophistication assumed by Captain Absolute's personal servant who wears a scarlet livery coat, light waistcoat and breeches. They pass each other and appear to be continuing on their several ways when Fag suddenly stops, whirls around, and calls back to the coachman.

FAG: *(stopping short)* What — Thomas! *(amazed at seeing him in Bath)* Sure 'tis he? *(turning and calling after the retreating figure)* What! — Thomas! — Thomas!

THOMAS: *(turning and recognizing Fag; heartily)* Hey! Odd's life — Mr. Fag! — give us your hand, my old fellow-servant.

FAG: *(entirely friendly, but showing awareness of the superiority and delicacy of his position as a gentleman's gentleman)* Excuse my glove, Thomas! — I'm devilish glad to see you, my lad. *(looking him over with benevolent concern)* Why, my prince of charioteers, you look as hearty! *(betraying his surprise)* But who the deuce thought of seeing you in Bath?

58

THOMAS: *(happy to oblige)* Sure, master, Madam Julia, Harry, Mrs. Kate, and the postillion be all come.

FAG: *(with well-bred astonishment)* Indeed!

THOMAS: *(delighted to be a source of information)* Aye, master thought another fit of the gout was coming to make him a visit; so he'd a mind to g't the slip, and whip! *(gesturing as if to whip up the horses)* — we were all off at an hour's warning.

FAG: *(ruminatively)* Aye, aye, hasty in everything, or it would not be Sir Anthony Absolute!

THOMAS: *(always interested in members of the family)* But tell us, Mr. Fag, how does young master? Odd![1] Sir Anthony will stare to see the Captain here!

FAG: *(with a surprising announcement of his own to make)* I do not serve Captain Absolute now.

THOMAS: *(uncomprehending)* Why sure!

FAG: At present I am employed by Ensign Beverley.

THOMAS: *(with obvious disapprobation)* I doubt, Mr. Fag, you ha'n't changed for the better.

FAG: *(enjoying his private riddle)* I have not changed, Thomas.

THOMAS: *(completely bewildered)* No! Why, didn't you say you had left young master?

FAG: *(with teasing precision)* No! *(relenting)* Well, honest Thomas, I must puzzle you no farther: — briefly then — Captain Absolute and Ensign Beverley are one and the same person.

THOMAS: *(factually)* The devil they are!

FAG: So it is indeed, Thomas; and the ensign half of my master being on guard at present — the captain has nothing to do with me.

THOMAS: *(painfully attentive and making a glimmer of sense out of Fag's enigmatic disclosure)* So, so! What, this is some freak, I warrant! *(anxiously)* Do tell us, Mr. Fag, the meaning o't — you know I ha' trusted you.

---

[1] A euphemism for *God*. The mild profanity throughout the play is similar: "Odd's life" (above), " 'Sdeath" (later) for *God's death,* and many more intricate variations.

FAG: *(severely)* You'll be secret, Thomas?

THOMAS: *(solemnly)* As a coach-horse.

FAG: *(with a dramatic flourish lost on but admired by his humble audience)* Why then the cause of all this is — Love, — Love, Thomas, who (as you may get read to you) has been a masquerader ever since the days of Jupiter.

THOMAS: *(his mental exertion causing him to frown)* Aye, aye; — I guessed there was a lady in the case: — but pray, why does your master pass only for ensign? Now if he had shammed general indeed —

FAG: *(cutting him off)* Ah! Thomas, there lies the mystery o' the matter. Hark'ee, Thomas, my master is in love with a lady of a very singular taste: a lady who likes him better as a half-pay ensign than if she knew he was son and heir to Sir Anthony Absolute, a baronet of three thousand a year.

THOMAS: That is an odd taste! *(eagerly)* But has she got the stuff, Mr. Fag? Is she rich, hey?

FAG: *(exploding)* Rich! Why, I believe she owns half the stocks! Zounds! Thomas, she could pay the national debt as easily as I could my washerwoman! She has a lapdog that eats out of gold, — she feeds her parrot with small pearls, — and all her thread-papers are made of banknotes!

THOMAS: *(with loyal enthusiasm)* Bravo, faith! — Odd! I warrant she has a set of thousands[2] at least: — but does she draw kindly with the captain?

FAG: As fond as pigeons.

THOMAS: *(humbly)* May one hear her name?

FAG: Miss Lydia Languish. But there is an old tough aunt in the way; though, by the by, she has never seen my master — for we got acquainted with Miss while on a visit in Gloucestershire.

THOMAS: *(heartily)* Well — I wish they were once harnessed together in matrony. *(resuming his tone of*

---

[2] A set usually consisted of six matched horses; hers worth thousands of pounds.

humility to his obvious superior) But pray, Mr. Fag, what kind of a place is this Bath? I ha' heard a deal of it — *(shaking his head)* Here's a mort[3] o' merry-making, hey?

FAG: *(with sophisticated condescension)* Pretty well, Thomas, pretty well — 'tis a good lounge; in the morning we go to the pumproom (though neither my master nor I drink the waters); after breakfast we saunter on the parades,[4] or play a game at billiards; at night we dance; but I'm tired of the place: their regular hours stupify me — not a fiddle nor a card after eleven! However, Mr. Faulkland's gentleman and I keep it up a little in private parties; — I'll introduce you there, Thomas — you'll like him much.

THOMAS: *(a broad smile exhibiting his pleasure at being included in this select circle)* Sure I know Mr. Du-Peigne — *(casually)* You know his master is to marry Madam Julia.

FAG: *(taken aback by the fact that the lowly Thomas could disclose anything to him and so resuming his air of superiority)* I had forgot. But, Thomas, you must polish a little — indeed you must. Here now — this wig! What the devil do you do with a wig, Thomas? None of the London whips of any degree of *ton*[5] wear wigs now.

THOMAS: *(heavily)* More's the pity! more's the pity, I say. Odd's life! when I heard how the lawyers and doctors had took to their own hair, I thought how 'twould go next: — odd rabbit it! when the fashion had got foot on the bar, I guessed 'twould mount to the box! *(querulously)* But 'tis all out of character, believe me, Mr. Fag: and look'ee, I'll never gi' up mine — the lawyers and doctors may do as they will.

FAG: *(placatingly)* Well, Thomas, we'll not quarrel about that.

THOMAS: *(unshaken from his horror of novelty)* Why,

---

[3] A great deal.

[4] Broad walks laid out for the promenading of Bath's fashionable visitors.

[5] Tone or class.

bless you, the gentlemen of the professions ben't all of
a mind — for in our village now, thoff[6] Jack Gauge, the
exciseman,[7] has ta'en to his carrots[8] there's little Dick the
farrier swears he'll never forsake his bob, though all the
college should appear with their own heads!

FAG: *(agreeing heartily to stop the flow of eloquence)*
Indeed! Well said, Dick! *(suddenly intent on something
in the distance)* But hold — *(pointing offstage)* Mark!
mark, Thomas.

THOMAS: Zooks![9] 'tis the captain. Is that the lady with
him?

FAG: *(peering)* No, no, that is Madam Lucy, my master's mistress's maid. They lodge at that house — *(suddenly remembering his duty)* But I must after him to tell
him the news.

THOMAS: *(so intently observing that he has barely
heard Fag's last remark)* Odd! he's giving her money!
*(but the remark does penetrate, so he turns to Fag in
leave-taking)* Well, Mr. Fag —

FAG: *(hurriedly)* Good-bye, Thomas. *(moving off in
the direction of his master)* I have an appointment in
Gyde's Porch[10] this evening at eight; meet me there, and
we'll make a little party. *(He disappears into the wings as
Thomas turns and resumes his walk offstage in the opposite direction.)*

Scene Two

*Lydia Languish's Dressing Room in the lodgings at Bath
rented by her aunt Mrs. Malaprop. The dressing table,
sofa, occasional chairs, and general decor of the room*

---

[6] Though.

[7] An officer who measured contents of casks.

[8] His own hair, presumably red.

[9] A popular abbreviation of *Gadzooks,* euphemism for *God's
hooks;* i.e., the nails of the cross.

[10] Mr. Gyde's rooms, garden, and retired walk on the edge of
the river were popular with society.

have the kind of faded elegance which Society was forced to put up with when vacationing in this resort. The opening of the scene reveals Lydia half-reclining on the sofa, languidly reading a book. Her dress, voluminously skirted and pinched at the waist, is made of a watered white fabric delicately embroidered with a narrow cerise cording, setting off her fresh young beauty of which she is very conscious. The book she is reading is one of a multitude of romantic and sentimental novels which have filled her head with such daydreams that she lives in a perpetual haze of romantic rapture. She therefore despises position, money, conventional marriage, and all the other humdrum practicalities of life. The immediate result of her infatuation has been to force the wealthy scion Captain Absolute to adopt the character of the lowly Ensign Beverley in order to woo her. Lucy, her coquettish and opportunistic personal maid, has just returned from her conversation with Captain Absolute, witnessed by the servants in the preceding scene.

LUCY: *(as if in answer to a rebuke by her mistress)* Indeed, ma'am, I traversed half the town in search of it: I don't believe there's a circulating library in Bath I ha'n't been at.

LYDIA: *(very much disappointed)* And could not you get *The Reward of Constancy?*

LUCY: *(protesting)* No, indeed, ma'am.

LYDIA: Nor *The Fatal Connexion?*

LUCY: No, indeed, ma'am.

LYDIA: Nor *The Mistakes of the Heart?*

LUCY: *(earnestly)* Ma'am, as ill luck would have it, Mr. Bull said Miss Sukey Saunter had just fetched it away.

LYDIA: *(sighing fatalistically)* Heigh-ho! *(betraying her exasperation)* Did you inquire for *The Delicate Distress?*

LUCY: *(making clear her devotion to her errand)* Or, *The Memoirs of Lady Woodford? (emphatically)* Yes, indeed, ma'am. I asked everywhere for it; and I might have brought it from Mr. Frederick's, but Lady Slattern Lounger, who had just sent it home, had so soiled and dog's-eared it, it wa'n't fit for a Christian to read.

LYDIA: *(defeated)* Heigh-ho! *(bitterly)* Yes, I always know when Lady Slattern has been before me. She has a most observing thumb; and I believe cherishes her nails for the convenience of making marginal notes. *(in a tone of enforced patience)* Well, child, what *have* you brought me?

LUCY: *(eagerly)* Oh! here, ma'am. *(digs into her pockets and beneath her cloak producing one by one the books as she names them)* This is *The Gordian Knot,* — and this *Peregrine Pickle.* Here are *The Tears of Sensibility,* and *Humphrey Clinker.* This is *The Memoirs of a Lady of Quality, written by herself,* and here the second volume of *The Sentimental Journey.*

LYDIA: *(resigning herself to make do with such books of sentiment and romance as seem to be available, though she has probably read some of them before)* Heigh-ho! *(looking toward the dressing table where a few books are scattered about near the mirror)* What are those books by the glass?

LUCY: The great one is only *The Whole Duty of Man,* where I press a few blonds,[1] ma'am.

LYDIA: *(sighing with boredom)* Very well — give me the sal volatile.

LUCY: *(ignorant of the technical and elegant term for smelling salts)* Is it in a blue cover, ma'am?

LYDIA: *(with exasperation)* My smelling-bottle, you simpleton!

LUCY: *(her face lighting up)* Oh, the drops! *(taking the bottle from the table)* Here, ma'am.

LYDIA: *(hearing sounds outside)* Hold! — here's some one coming. *(delighted at the prospect of company)* Quick! see who it is. *(Lucy goes out to the left.)* Surely, I heard my cousin Julia's voice.

---

[1] This well-known religious tome by Jeremy Taylor is being used only to straighten out lacey nets used as scarfs to throw over bare shoulders.

Ah, Julia, I have a thousand things to tell you!

LUCY: *(poking her head back through the door)* Lud! ma'am, here is Miss Melville.

LYDIA: *(delighted)* Is it possible! *(opens her arms to embrace her dearest friend. Julia enters exhibiting equal delight. She is a trifle plainer than Lydia and, although romantic at heart, she possesses an innate solid honesty and sense of reality which has prevented her being carried away, like Lydia, by the romantic extravagances currently in fashion.)* My dearest Julia, how delighted am I! *(They embrace rapturously)* How unexpected was this happiness!

JULIA: *(radiantly)* True, Lydia — and our pleasure is the greater. But what has been the matter? —you were denied to me at first.

LYDIA: *(sighing)* Ah, Julia, I have a thousand things to tell you! *(But her curiosity is stronger than her misery at being confined to her quarters to prevent her from meeting Beverley again.)* But first inform me what has conjured you to Bath? Is Sir Anthony here?

JULIA: *(somewhat breathless with excitement)* He is — we are arrived within this hour! — and I suppose he will be here to wait on Mrs. Malaprop as soon as he is dressed.

LYDIA: Then before we are interrupted, let me impart to you some of my distress! *(dramatically)* I know your gentle nature will sympathize with me, though your prudence will condemn me! My letters have informed you of my whole connection with Beverley; but I have lost him, Julia! My aunt has discovered our intercourse by a note she intercepted, and has confined me ever since! Yet, would you believe it? she has absolutely fallen in love with a tall Irish baronet she met one night since we have been here, at Lady Macshuffle's rout.[2]

JULIA: *(unbelieving)* You jest, Lydia!

LYDIA: *(seriously)* No, upon my word. She really carries on a kind of correspondence with him, under a feigned name, though, till she chooses to be known to him — *(indicating her awareness that her aunt is also*

---

[2] A social gathering.

a victim of romantic sentimentalism by guessing that she is using a pen name celebrated in love poetry) But it is a Delia or a Celia, I assure you.

JULIA: Then, surely, she is now more indulgent to her niece.

LYDIA: Quite the contrary. Since she has discovered her own frailty, she is become more suspicious of mine. *(recalling that her aunt does favor the suitor she despises)* Then I must inform you of another plague! That odious Acres is to be in Bath to-day; so that I protest I shall be teased out of all spirits!

JULIA: *(cheerfully)* Come, come, Lydia, hope for the best — Sir Anthony shall use his interest with Mrs. Malaprop.

LYDIA: *(so preoccupied with her own distress that she has scarcely heard)* But you have not heard the worst. Unfortunately I had quarreled with my poor Beverley, just before my aunt made the discovery, and I have not seen him since, to make it up.

JULIA: *(with great curiosity)* What was his offence?

LYDIA: *(her expression sad and inviting sympathy)* Nothing at all! — But, I don't know how it was, as often as we had been together, we had never had a quarrel! And somehow, I was afraid he would never give me an opportunity. So, last Thursday, I wrote a letter to myself, to inform myself that Beverley was at that time paying his addresses to another woman. I signed it *your friend unknown,* showed it to Beverley, charged him with his falsehood, put myself in a violent passion, and vowed I'd never see him more.

JULIA: *(with pained surprise)* And you let him depart so, and have not seen him since?

LYDIA: *(appreciative of a sympathetic listener)* 'Twas the next day my aunt found the matter out. I intended only to have teased him three days and a half — *(with dramatic anguish)* — and now I've lost him forever.

JULIA: *(comfortingly)* If he is as deserving and sincere as you have represented him to me, he will never give you up so. *(attempting to inject a note of reason)* Yet consider, Lydia, you tell me he is but an ensign, and you have thirty thousand pounds!

LYDIA: *(bathed in the glow of her exquisite romanticism)* But you know I lose most of my fortune if I marry without my aunt's consent, till of age; and that is what I have determined to do, ever since I knew the penalty. Nor could I love the man who would wish to wait a day for the alternative.

JULIA: *(reprovingly)* Nay, this is caprice!

LYDIA: *(sharply)* What, does Julia tax me with caprice? — I thought her lover Faulkland had inured her to it.

JULIA: *(sensibly)* I do not love even *his* faults.

LYDIA: *(very much interested in her friend's affair)* But apropos — You have sent to him, I suppose?

JULIA: Not yet, upon my word — nor has he the least idea of my being in Bath. Sir Anthony's resolution was so sudden, I could not inform him of it.

LYDIA: Well, Julia, you are your own mistress (though under the protection of Sir Anthony), yet have you, for this long year, been a slave to the caprice, the whim, the jealousy of this ungrateful Faulkland, who will ever delay assuming the right of a husband, while you suffer him to be equally imperious as a lover.

JULIA: *(defensively)* Nay, you are wrong entirely. We were contracted before my father's death. That, and some consequent embarrassments, have delayed what I know to be my Faulkland's most ardent wish. He is too generous to trifle on such a point — and for his character, you wrong him there too. No, Lydia, he is too proud, too noble to be jealous; if he is captious, 'tis without dissembling; if fretful, without rudeness. Unused to the fopperies of love, he is negligent of the little duties expected from a lover — but being unhackneyed in the passion, his affection is ardent and sincere, and as it engrosses his whole soul, he expects every thought and emotion of his mistress to move in unison with his. Yet, though his pride calls for this full return, his humility makes him undervalue those qualities in him which would entitle him to it; and not feeling why he should be loved to the degree he wishes, he still suspects that he is not loved enough. This temper, I must own, has cost me many unhappy hours; but I have learned to think myself his debtor, for those imperfections which arise from the ardour of his attachment.

LYDIA: *(conciliatingly)* Well, I cannot blame you for defending him. But tell me candidly, Julia, had he never saved your life, do you think you should have been attached to him as you are? Believe me, the rude blast that overset your boat was a prosperous gale of love to him.

JULIA: *(with gentle earnestness)* Gratitude may have strengthened my attachment to Mr. Faulkland, but I loved him before he had preserved me; yet surely that alone were an obligation sufficient.

LYDIA: *(spiritedly)* Obligation! why a water spaniel would have done as much! Well, I should never think of giving my heart to a man because he could swim!

JULIA: Come, Lydia, you are too inconsiderate.

LYDIA: *(relenting)* Nay, I do but jest. *(seeing Lucy suddenly put in an appearance at the door)* What's here?

LUCY: *(breathlessly)* O ma'am here is Sir Anthony Absolute just come home with your aunt.

LYDIA: *(with determination)* They'll not come here. — Lucy, do you watch. *(Lucy disappears from the doorway.)*

JULIA: *(nervously)* Yet *I* must go. Sir Anthony does not know I am here, and if we meet, he'll detain me, to show me the town. I'll take another opportunity of paying my respects to Mrs. Malaprop, when she shall treat me, as long as she chooses, with her select words so ingeniously *misapplied,* without being mispronounced.

(Lucy suddenly reappears and enters in a flurry.)

LUCY: O Lud! ma'am, they are both coming upstairs.

LYDIA: *(speaking rapidly)* Well, I'll not detain you, coz. — Adieu, my dear Julia, I'm sure you are in haste to send to Faulkland. *(pointing to the opposite door at the right of the room)* There — through my room you'll find another staircase.

JULIA: Adieu! *(hurriedly embraces Lydia and leaves.)*

LYDIA: *(turning to Lucy with no indication of panic but speaking with rapid efficiency)* Here, my dear Lucy, hide these books. Quick, quick! — Fling *Peregrine Pickle* under the toilet — throw *Roderick Random* into the closet — put *The Innocent Adultery* into *The Whole Duty of Man* — thrust *Lord Aimworth* under the sofa — cram *Ovid* behind the bolster — there — put *The Man of Feeling* into your pocket — so, so — now lay *Mrs. Chapone* in sight, and leave *Fordyce's Sermons* open on the table.

LUCY: *(following directions as they are given and coming at last to* Fordyce's Sermons *which she opens)* O burn it, ma'am! the hairdresser has torn away as far as *Proper Pride.*

LYDIA: Never mind — open at *Sobriety.* — Fling me *Lord Chesterfield's Letters.* *(looking militantly toward the door)* Now for 'em.

Lucy retires to Lydia's bedroom as Mrs. Malaprop and Sir Anthony Absolute enter through the outer door. Mrs. Malaprop, inclined to plumpness, gives a decidedly matronly appearance. Although pleased with the elegance of her dress, she has rather uncertain taste with a preference for large figured patterns which, coupled with a figure of her own that refuses to conform to the fashions of the period, creates a general impression of dowdiness. Sir Anthony is immediately typed as a well-fed brusque John Bullish sort of Devonshire squire, conservative, dogmatic, wealthy, and accustomed to being treated with respect despite his transcendent absurdity. His light blue suit lined with crimson silk, his black silk plush cuffs, his cocked hat with gold loop and cordage all add to this general impression of the majestic dullard.

MRS. MALAPROP: *(pointing dramatically at Lydia and speaking with vehemence)* There, Sir Anthony, — sits the *deliberate* simpleton who wants to disgrace her family, and lavish herself on a fellow not worth a shilling.

LYDIA: *(coldly)* Madam, I thought you once —

MRS. MALAPROP: *(interrupting violently)* You *thought,*

miss! I don't know any business you have to think at all
— *(laying down an obvious maxim)* — Thought does
not become a young woman. *(with dignified precision)*
But the point we would request of you is, that you will
promise to forget this fellow — to *illiterate*[3] him, I say,
quite from your memory.

LYDIA: *(replying quietly but firmly with a sentimental
maxim of her own)* Ah, madam! our memories are in-
dependent of our wills. It is not so easy to forget.

MRS. MALAPROP: *(with angry insistence)* But I say it
is, miss; there is nothing on earth so easy as to forget,
if a person chooses to set about it. I'm sure I have as
much forgot your poor dear uncle as if he had never
existed — and I thought it my duty so to do; *(sharply)*
and let me tell you Lydia, these violent memories don't
become a young woman.

SIR ANTHONY: *(utterly amazed at this display of youthful disobedience)* Why sure she won't pretend to remember what she's ordered not! *(with an air of authoritative
certainty)* Aye, this comes of her reading!

LYDIA: *(ignoring him)* What crime, madam, have I
committed, to be treated thus?

MRS. MALAPROP: Now don't attempt to extirpate[4]
yourself from the matter; you know I have proof con-
trovertible[5] of it. — But tell me, will you promise to do
as you're bid? Will you take a husband of your friends'
choosing?

LYDIA: *(with high-souled antagonism)* Madam, I must
tell you plainly, that had I no preference for any one else,
the choice you have made would be my aversion.

MRS. MALAPROP: *(heavily)* What business have you,
miss, with *preference* and *aversion*? They don't become
a young woman; and you ought to know, that as both
always wear off, 'tis safest in matrimony to begin with
a little aversion. I am sure I hated your poor dear uncle

---

[3] She means, of course, *obliterate*. This is the first of her many
malapropisms.

[4] She probably means *extricate*.

[5] *incontrovertible*.

before marriage as if he'd been a blackamoor — and yet, miss, you are sensible what a wife I made! — and when it pleased Heaven to release me from him, 'tis unknown what tears I shed! *(relenting so far as to be willing to bargain)* But suppose we were going to give you another choice, will you promise to give up this Beverley?

LYDIA: *(still romantically transcendental)* Could I belie my thoughts so far as to give that promise, my actions would certainly as far belie my words.

MRS. MALAPROP: *(flaring up again in utter outrage)* Take yourself to your room! You are fit company for nothing but your own ill-humors.

LYDIA: Willingly, ma'am — *(with an air of noble martyrdom)* — I cannot change for the worse. *(She makes a dignified exit to her room.)*

MRS. MALAPROP: *(turning to Sir Anthony for sympathy)* There's a little intricate[6] hussy for you!

SIR ANTHONY: *(with his usual blunt air of authority)* It is not to be wondered at, ma'am — all this is the natural consequence of teaching girls to read. Had I a thousand daughters, by Heaven! — I'd as soon have them taught the black art as their alphabet!

MRS. MALAPROP: *(chiding him gently, and aware of her own notion of herself as being a woman of learning)* Nay, nay, Sir Anthony, you are an absolute misanthropy.[7]

SIR ANTHONY: *(illustrating the unquestionable validity of his beliefs)* In my way hither, Mrs. Malaprop, I observed your niece's maid coming forth from a circulating library! She had a book in each hand — they were half-bound volumes with marble covers! From that moment I guessed how full of duty I should see her mistress!

MRS. MALAPROP: *(shaken)* Those are vile places, indeed!

SIR ANTHONY: *(sententiously)* Madam, a circulating library in a town is as an evergreen tree of diabolical knowledge! It blossoms through the year! And depend on

6 *Obstinate?*
7 *Misanthrope* or *misanthropist*.

it, Mrs. Malaprop, that they who are so fond of handling the leaves, will long for the fruit at last.

MRS. MALAPROP: *(almost blushing)* Fie, fie, Sir Anthony, you surely speak laconically.[8]

SIR ANTHONY: Why, Mrs. Malaprop, in moderation, now, what would *you* have a woman know?

MRS. MALAPROP: *(somewhat cowed but eager to display her intellectuality)* Observe me, Sir Anthony. I would by no means wish a daughter of mine to be a progeny[9] of learning; I don't think so much learning becomes a *young woman;* for instance, I would never let her meddle with Greek, or Hebrew, or algebra, or simony, or fluxions, or paradoxes,[10] or such inflammatory branches of learning — neither would it be necessary for her to handle any of your mathematical, astronomical, diabolical[11] instruments. — But, Sir Anthony, I would send her, at nine years old, to a boarding-school, in order to learn a little ingenuity and artifice.[12] Then, sir, she should have a supercilious[13] knowledge in accounts; — and as she grew up, I would have her instructed in geometry,[14] that she might know something of the contagious[15] countries; — but above all, Sir Anthony, she should be mistress of orthodoxy,[16] that she might not misspell, and mis-pronounce words so shamefully as girls usually do; and likewise that she might reprehend[17] the true meaning of what she is saying. This, Sir Anthony, is what I would have a woman know; *(with deep conviction)* — And I don't think there is a superstitious[18] article in it.

---

[8] *Sardonically* or *ironically?*

[9] *Prodigy.*

[10] Could she have meant *algebra, or geometry, or functions, or parabolas?*

[11] *Dialectical?*

[12] *Artistry?*

[13] *Superficial.*

[14] *Geography.*

[15] *Contiguous?*

[16] *Orthography.*

[17] *Comprehend.*

[18] *Superfluous.*

SIR ANTHONY: *(unable to conceal his amusement at her malapropisms)* Well, well, Mrs. Malaprop, I will dispute the point no further with you; though I must confess that you are a truly moderate and polite arguer, for almost every third word you say is on my side of the question. *(seriously)* But, Mrs. Malaprop, to the more important point in debate — you say you have no objection to my proposal?

MRS. MALAPROP: *(good-humoredly)* None, I assure you. I am under no positive engagement with Mr. Acres, and as Lydia is so obstinate against him, perhaps your son may have better success.

SIR ANTHONY: *(pleased)* Well, madam, I will write for the boy directly. He knows not a syllable of this yet, though I have for some time had the proposal in my head. He is at present with his regiment.

MRS. MALAPROP: We have never seen your son, Sir Anthony; but I hope no objection on his side.

SIR ANTHONY: *(brushing off such a preposterous supposition)* Objection! — let him object if he dare! No, no, Mrs. Malaprop, Jack knows that the least demur puts me in a frenzy directly. My process was always very simple — in their younger days, 'twas "Jack, do this;" — if he demurred, I knocked him down — and if he grumbled at that, I always sent him out of the room.

MRS. MALAPROP: *(nodding her head vigorously)* Aye, and the properest way, o' my conscience! *(with gravity)* Nothing is so conciliating to young people as severity. *(politely dismissing her guest)* Well, Sir Anthony, I shall give Mr. Acres his discharge, and prepare Lydia to receive your son's invocations;[19] — and I hope you will represent her to the captain as an object not altogether illegible.[20]

SIR ANTHONY: *(taking his leave)* Madam, I will handle the subject prudently. — Well, I must leave you; and let me beg you, Mrs. Malaprop, to enforce this matter roundly to the girl. — Take my advice — keep a tight

---

[19] *Addresses.*
[20] *Ineligible.*

Objection!——let him object if he dare!

hand; if she rejects this proposal, clap her under lock and key; and if you were just to let the servants forget to bring her dinner for three or four days, you can't conceive how she'd come about. *(He bows and leaves.)*

MRS. MALAPROP: *(alone; brooding aloud)* Well, at any rate, I shall be glad to get her from under my intuition.[21] She has somehow discovered my partiality for Sir Lucius O'Trigger — sure, Lucy can't have betrayed me! No, the girl is such a simpleton, I should have made her confess it. *(calling through the bedroom door)* Lucy! — Lucy! *(resuming her soliloquy)* Had she been one of your artificial[22] ones, I should never have trusted her.

LUCY: *(entering)* Did you call, ma'am?

MRS. MALAPROP: Yes, girl. — Did you see Sir Lucius while you was out?

LUCY: *(dutifully)* No, indeed, ma'am, not a glimpse of him.

MRS. MALAPROP: *(suspiciously)* You are sure, Lucy, that you never mentioned —

LUCY: *(hurt at the bare suggestion)* Oh gemini! I'd sooner cut my tongue out.

MRS. MALAPROP: *(drily)* Well, don't let your simplicity be imposed on.

LUCY: No, ma'am.

MRS. MALAPROP: *(pleasantly)* So, come to me presently, and I'll give you another letter to Sir Lucius; — *(severely)* But mind, Lucy — if ever you betray what you are entrusted with (unless it be other people's secrets to me) you forfeit my malevolence[23] forever; and your being a simpleton shall be no excuse for your locality.[24] *(She departs majestically through the outer door.)*

LUCY: *(giggling to herself)* Ha! ha! ha! *(altering her simple subservient manner abruptly to one of arch knowingness)* So, my dear Simplicity, let me give you a little respite. Let girls in my station be as fond of appearing

---

21 *Tuition.*
22 *Artful.*
23 *Benevolence.*
24 *Loquacity.*

expert and knowing in their trusts; commend *me* to a mask of silliness, and a pair of sharp eyes for my own interest under it! Let me see to what account have I turned my simplicity lately. *(pulls a small memo book from her pocket and looks at it)* For *abetting Miss Lydia Languish in a design of running away with an Ensign!* — *in money — sundry times — twelve pounds twelve — gowns, five — hats, ruffles, caps, etc., etc. — numberless! From the said Ensign, within this last month, six guineas and a half.* About a quarter's pay! Item, *from Mrs. Malaprop, for betraying the young people to her —* when I found matters were likely to be discovered — *two guineas, and a black paduasoy.*[25] Item, *from Mr. Acres, for carrying divers letters —* which I never delivered — *two guineas, and a pair of buckles.* Item, *from Sir Lucius O'Trigger — three gowns — two gold pocket-pieces — and a silver snuffbox!* Well done, Simplicity! Yet I was forced to make my Hibernian believe that he was corresponding, not with the aunt, but with the niece: for though not over-rich, I found he had too much pride and delicacy to sacrifice the feelings of a gentleman to the necessities of his fortune. *(She readjusts her features to their habitual non-committal moronic expression and goes out through the door to Lydia's room.)*

---

[25] A garment made of a particular type of smooth, rich silk — Padua silk.

ACT TWO
Scene One

The drawing room in Captain Absolute's suite in Bath. Not as elegant as Mrs. Malaprop's lodgings, the room nevertheless indicates that it is rented only to wealthy Society vacationers. Captain Absolute, masquerading in Bath as Ensign Beverley (wearing a scarlet regimental dress coat and white breeches), is a handsome young man whose sense of humor gives added charm to his military bearing. As the scene opens, he is talking to his man Fag who is considerably less jaunty with his master than he was with the coachman in the opening scene of the play.

FAG: *(continuing his revelation to Captain Absolute that his father, Sir Anthony, has just arrived in Bath)* Sir, while I was there, Sir Anthony came in: I told him you had sent me to inquire after his health, and to know if he was at leisure to see you.

CAPTAIN ABSOLUTE: *(amused at Fag's faithful cleverness)* And what did he say, on hearing I was at Bath?

FAG: Sir, in my life I never saw an elderly gentleman more astonished! He started back two or three paces, rapped out a dozen interjectural oaths, and asked what the devil had brought you here!

CAPTAIN ABSOLUTE: Well, sir, and what did you say?

FAG: *(casually)* Oh, I lied, sir — I forget the precise lie; but you may depend on't, he got no truth from me. *(with a worried expression)* Yet, with submission, for fear of blunders in future, I should be glad to fix what *has* brought us to Bath: in order that we may lie a little

78

consistently. Sir Anthony's servants were curious, sir, very curious indeed.

CAPTAIN ABSOLUTE: *(suspiciously)* You have said nothing to them?

FAG: *(protesting)* Oh, not a word, sir, — not a word! Mr. Thomas, indeed, the coachman (whom I take to be the discreetest of whips) —

CAPTAIN ABSOLUTE: *(with annoyance)* 'Sdeath — you rascal! you have not trusted him!

FAG: *(placatingly)* Oh, no, sir — no — no — not a syllable, upon my veracity! *(with pride in his own cleverness)* He was, indeed, a little inquisitive; but I was sly, sir — devilish sly! "My master," said I, "honest Thomas," — you know, sir, one says *honest* to one's inferiors — "is come to Bath to recruit." Yes, sir, I said to recruit — *(snidely)* and whether for men, money, or constitution, you know, sir, is nothing to him, nor any one else.

CAPTAIN ABSOLUTE: *(not at all interested in the details)* Well, recruit will do — let it be so.

FAG: *(enthusiastically)* Oh, sir, recruit will do surprisingly — indeed, to give the thing an air, I told Thomas that your honor had already enlisted five disbanded chairmen,[1] seven minority waiters,[2] and thirteen billiardmarkers.

CAPTAIN ABSOLUTE: You Blockhead, never say more than is necessary.

FAG: *(with great deference)* I beg pardon, sir — I beg pardon — but, with submission, a lie is nothing unless one supports it. Sir, whenever I draw on my invention for a good current lie, I always forge indorsements as well as the bill.

CAPTAIN ABSOLUTE: *(drily)* Well, take care you don't hurt your credit by offering too much security. *(closing the subject)* Is Mr. Faulkland returned?

---

[1] Bearers of sedan chairs.

[2] Fag is exhibiting his devilish cleverness by using the military term *disbanded* and the political epithet *minority* to describe attendants at Bath who are unemployed.

FAG: *(subdued)* He is above, sir, changing his dress.

CAPTAIN ABSOLUTE: Can you tell whether he has been informed of Sir Anthony's and Miss Melville's arrival?

FAG: I fancy not, sir; he has seen no one since he came in but his gentleman, who was with him at Bristol — *(cocking his ear toward the doorway at the right)* — I think sir, I hear Mr. Faulkland coming down —

CAPTAIN ABSOLUTE: *(with crisp authority)* Go. — Tell him I am here.

FAG: *(smartly)* Yes, sir. *(starts toward the door, but turns almost immediately and condescends to his master)* I beg pardon, sir, but should Sir Anthony call, you will do me the favor to remember that we are *recruiting,* if you please.

CAPTAIN ABSOLUTE: *(showing his impatience at Fag's delaying)* Well, well.

FAG: *(pleadingly but with determination to make Captain Absolute aware of the importance of these details which he has seemed so unimpressed with)* And, in tenderness to my character, if your honor could bring in the chairmen and waiters, I should esteem it as an obligation; for though I never scruple a lie to serve my master, yet it hurts one's conscience to be found out. *(He does not wait for a reply, for the expression of mounting annoyance on his master's face is enough to make him turn again and make a rapid exit.)*

CAPTAIN ABSOLUTE: *(instantly relaxing his expression which was assumed principally for Fag's benefit, and smiling in anticipation of needling his friend Faulkland whose painfully involved love for Julia makes him an easy victim)* Now for my whimsical friend — if he does not know that his mistress is here, I'll tease him a little before I tell him — *(Faulkland enters — soberly clad in a dark brown dress coat, white waistcoat, and black silk breeches and stockings — and is greeted with sincere cordiality)* — Faulkland, you're welcome to Bath again; you are punctual in your return.

FAULKLAND: *(with equal cordiality)* Yes; I had nothing to detain me, when I had finished the business I went on. Well, what news since I left you? How stand matters between you and Lydia?

CAPTAIN ABSOLUTE: *(lightly)* Faith, much as they were; I have not seen her since our quarrel; however, I expect to be recalled every hour.

FAULKLAND: *(unable to comprehend such a relaxed attitude toward an affair of the heart)* Why don't you persuade her to go off with you at once? Hasty-impatient

CAPTAIN ABSOLUTE: *(with exaggerated amazement at such an absurd suggestion)* What, and lose two-thirds of her fortune? You forget that, my friend. No, no, I could have brought her to that long ago. Does he really love her

FAULKLAND: *(with deep earnestness and concern)* Nay, then, you trifle too long — if you are sure of her, propose to the aunt in your own character, and write to Sir Anthony for his consesnt.

CAPTAIN ABSOLUTE: *(checking this tempestuous enthusiasm)* Softly, softly; for though I am convinced my little Lydia would elope with me as Ensign Beverley, yet am I by no means certain that she would take me with the impediment of our friends' consent, a regular humdrum wedding, and the reversion of a good fortune on my side; no, no; I must prepare her gradually for the discovery, and make myself necessary to her before I risk it. *(dismissing the subject)* Well, but, Faulkland, you'll dine with us today at the hotel?

FAULKLAND: *(gloomily, in the manner of the heavy, humorless love-hero)* Indeed I cannot; I am not in spirits to be of such a party.

CAPTAIN ABSOLUTE: *(rallying him)* By Heavens! I shall forswear your company. You are the most teasing, captious, incorrigible lover! — Do love like a man. appearance

FAULKNER: *(miserably)* I own I am unfit for company.

CAPTAIN ABSOLUTE: *(heartily but with a trace of annoyance)* Am I not a lover; aye, and a romantic one too? Yet do I carry everywhere with me such a confounded farrago of doubts, fears, hopes, wishes, and all the flimsy furniture of a country miss's brain!

FAULKNER: *(tragically and soulfully precious, superior*

to his earth-bound friend) Ah! Jack, your heart and soul
are not, like mine, fixed immutably on one only object.
You throw for a large stake, but losing, you could stake
and throw again: — but I have set my sum of happiness
on this cast, and not to succeed, were to be stripped of all.

CAPTAIN ABSOLUTE:*(as if completely out of patience)*
But, for Heaven's sake! what grounds for apprehension
can your whimsical brain conjure up at present?

FAULKLAND: *(distraught yet eager to tread the path
of the bleeding heart)* What grounds for apprehension,
did you say? Heavens! are there not a thousand! I fear
for her spirits — her health — her life. — My absence
may fret her; her anxiety for my return, her fears for
me, may oppress her gentle temper. And for her health,
does not every hour bring me causes to be alarmed? If
it rains, some shower may even then have chilled her
delicate frame! If the wind be keen, some rude blast may
have affected her! The heat of noon, the dews of the
evening, may endanger the life of her, for whom only I
value mine. Oh, Jack! when delicate and feeling souls
are separated, there is not a feature in the sky, not a
movement of the elements, not an aspiration of the
breeze, but hints some cause for a lover's apprehension!

CAPTAIN ABSOLUTE: *(matter-of-factly and in Dr. Johnson's best style of sound British sense.)* Aye, but we may
choose whether we will take the hint or not. — So, then
Faulkland, if you were convinced that Julia were well
and in spirits, you would be entirely content?

FAULKLAND: *(soulfully)* I should be happy beyond
measure — I am anxious only for that.

CAPTAIN ABSOLUTE: *(crisply)* Then to cure your anxiety at once — Miss Melville is in perfect health, and is
at this moment in Bath.

FAULKLAND:*(hurt and pleading)* Nay, Jack — don't
trifle with me.

CAPTAIN ABSOLUTE: She is arrived here with my father
within this hour.

FAULKLAND: *(brightening)* Can you be serious?

CAPTAIN ABSOLUTE: I thought you knew Sir Anthony

better than to be surprised at a sudden whim of this kind.
Seriously then, it is as I tell you — upon my honor.

FAULKLAND: *(ecstatically)* My dear friend! *(calling to
his servant)* Hollo, Du-Peigne! my hat. *(gratefully)* My
dear Jack — now nothing on earth can give me a moment's uneasiness.

FAG: *(entering to announce a visitor)* Sir, Mr. Acres,
just arrived, is below.

CAPTAIN ABSOLUTE: Stay, Faulkland, this Acres lives
within a mile of Sir Anthony, and he shall tell you how
your mistress has been ever since you left her. Fag, show
the gentleman up. *(Fag nods and leaves.)*

FAULKLAND: *(jealous of another man's proximity to
his beloved)* What, is he much acquainted in the family?

CAPTAIN ABSOLUTE: *(deliberately teasing)* Oh, very
intimate: I insist on your not going: besides, his character will divert you.

FAULKLAND: *(with nervous uncertainty)* Well, I should
like to ask him a few questions.

CAPTAIN ABSOLUTE: He is likewise a rival of mine —
that is, of my other self's, for he does not think his friend
Captain Absolute ever saw the lady in question; and it is
ridiculous enough to hear him complain to me of one
Beverley, a concealed skulking rival, who —

FAULKLAND: *(stopping him)* Hush! — he's here.

*Bob Acres erupts into the room. Lydia's formal suitor
— until Sir Anthony in the last scene proposed his son
to Mrs. Melaprop — is actually a rather immature country boy who is desperately attemping to present the appearance of a man of the world. His flashy riding coat,
white cord breeches, black boots, and gaudy jockey cap
make Captain Absolute and Faulkland seem sober by
comparison. He speaks rapidly and as if conscious of
the dazzling effect which his fashionable brilliance should
produce.*

ACRES: Ha! my dear friend, noble captain, and honest
Jack, how do'st thou? just arrived, faith, as you see. *(with
an exaggerated bow)* Sir, your humble servant. *(explosively)* Warm work on the roads, Jack! Odds whips and

wheels! I've travelled like a comet, with a tail of dust all the way as long as the Mall.

CAPTAIN ABSOLUTE: *(seemingly impressed)* Ah! Bob, you are indeed an eccentric planet, but we know your attraction hither. *(turning toward Faulkland)* Give me leave to introduce Mr. Faulkland to you; Mr. Faulkland, Mr. Acres.

ACRES: *(with formal stiffness)* Sir, I am most heartily glad to see you. Sir, I solicit your connections — *(with sudden realization)* Hey, Jack — what, this is Mr. Faulkland, who —

CAPTAIN ABSOLUTE: Aye, Bob, Miss Melville's Mr. Faulkland.

ACRES: *(exclaiming)* Odso! she and your father can be but just arrived before me — I suppose you have seen them. Ah! Mr. Faulkland, you are indeed a happy man.

FAULKLAND: I have not seen Miss Melville, yet, sir. *(anxiously)* I hope she enjoyed full health and spirits in Devonshire?

ACRES: *(enthusiastically)* Never knew her better in my life, sir, — never better. Odds blushes and blooms! She has been as healthy as the German Spa.

FAULKLAND: *(hurt)* Indeed! — I did hear that she had been a little indisposed.

ACRES: *(heartily)* False, false, sir — only said to vex you: quite the reverse, I assure you.

FAULKLAND: *(to Captain Absolute)* There, Jack, you see she had the advantage of me; I had almost fretted myself ill.

CAPTAIN ABSOLUTE: *(amused)* Now you are angry with your mistress for *not* having been sick.

FAULKLAND: *(fretfully)* No, no, you misunderstand me: yet surely a little trifling indisposition is not an unnatural consequence of absence from those we love. Now confess — isn't there something unkind in this violent, robust, unfeeling health?

CAPTAIN ABSOLUTE: *(in ironic agreement)* Oh, it was very unkind of her to be well in your absence, to be sure!

ACRES: *(a bit miffed at this private conversation which excludes him)* Good apartments, Jack.

FAULKLAND: *(ignoring the observation and determined to drain the dregs of his anguish; turning to Acres)* Well, sir, but you was saying that Miss Melville has been so *exceedingly* well — what, then, she has been merry and gay, I suppose? — Always in spirits — hey?

ACRES: *(emphatically)* Merry, odds crickets! she has been the belle and spirit of the company wherever she has been — so lively and entertaining! so full of wit and humor!

FAULKLAND: *(despairingly)* There, Jack, there. — Oh, by my soul! there is an innate levity in woman, that nothing can overcome. *(tragically)* What! happy, and I away.

CAPTAIN ABSOLUTE: *(laughing)* Have done. How foolish this is! just now you were only apprehensive for your mistress' spirits.

FAULKLAND: *(aggrieved)* Why, Jack, have *I* been the spirit of the company?

CAPTAIN ABSOLUTE: *(in emphatic agreement)* No, indeed, you have not.

FAULKLAND: Have *I* been lively and entertaining?

CAPTAIN ABSOLUTE: Oh, upon my word, I acquit you.

FAULKLAND: Have *I* been full of wit and humor?

CAPTAIN ABSOLUTE: No, faith, to do you justice, you have been confoundedly stupid indeed.

ACRES: *(to Captain Absolute)* What's the matter with the gentleman?

CAPTAIN ABSOLUTE: *(as if explaining the obvious)* He is only expressing satisfaction at hearing that Julia has been so well and happy — that's all — hey, Faulkland?

FAULKLAND: *(protesting)* Oh! I *am* rejoiced to hear it — yes, yes, she has a *happy* disposition!

ACRES: *(vigorously with simple unawareness of the real effects of his disclosures)* That she has indeed. — Then she is so accomplished — so sweet a voice — so expert at her harpsichord — such a mistress of flat and sharp, squallante, rumblante, and quiverante! There was this time month — odds ninums and crochets!³ how she did chirrup at Mrs. Piano's concert!

FAULKLAND: *(to Captain Absolute)* There again, what say you to this? You see she has been all mirth and song — *(pathetically)* — and not a thought of me!

CAPTAIN ABSOLUTE: Pho! man, is not music the food of love?

FAULKLAND: *(uncertainly)* Well, well, it may be so. *(to Acres)* Pray, Mr. ——— *(unnerved; to Captain Absolute)* — What's his damned name? — *(to Acres)* Do you remember what songs Miss Melville sung?

ACRES: *(his brow furrowing in painful thought)* Not I, indeed.

CAPTAIN ABSOLUTE: *(pretending deep thoughtfulness and seriousness)* Stay, now, they were some pretty melancholy purling-stream airs, I warrant; perhaps you may recollect; did she sing *When absent from my soul's delight?*

ACRES: *(shaking his head)* No, that wa'n't it.

CAPTAIN ABSOLUTE: Or, *Go, gentle gales!* *(singing)* *Go, gentle gales!*

ACRES: *(with deep seriousness)* Oh, no! nothing like it. *(his face suddenly lighting)* Odds! now I recollect one of them — *(singing boisterously)* *My heart's my own, my will is free.*

FAULKLAND: *(overwhelmed)* Fool! fool that I am! to fix my happiness on such a trifler! 'Sdeath! to make herself the pipe and ballad-monger of a circle! to soothe her light heart with catches and glees! *(to Captain Absolute)* What can you say to this, sir?

CAPTAIN ABSOLUTE: *(with mock earnestness)* Why, that I should be glad to hear my mistress had been so merry, sir.

FAULKLAND: *(protesting the imputation that his love is entirely selfish and trying to explain the inexplicable)* Nay, nay, nay — I'm *not* sorry that she has been happy — no, no, I am *glad* of that — I would not have her sad or sick; *(plaintively)* yet surely a sympathetic heart would

---

³ A combination of actual and nonsensical musical terms.

have shown itself even in the choice of a song — she
might have been *temperately* healthy, and somehow
plaintively gay; *(bitterly)* but she has been dancing too,
I doubt not!

ACRES: *(as if having been momentarily distracted)*
What does the gentleman say about dancing?

CAPTAIN ABSOLUTE: *(as if conveying information of
great importance)* He says the lady we speak of dances
as well as she sings.

ACRES: *(with the eagerness of the simple to communi-
cate)* Aye, truly, does she — there was at our last race
ball —

FAULKLAND: *(shouting him down)* There! there — I
told you so! I told you so! Oh! she thrives in my absence!
Dancing! but her whole feelings have been in opposition
with mine. *(in anguish)* I have been anxious, silent, pensive, sedentary — my days have been hours of care, my
nights of watchfulness — *(emphasizing every word of his
condemnation)* She has been all health! spirit! laugh!
song! dance! *(as if delivering a soliloquy from Hamlet)*
Oh! damned, *damned* levity!

CAPTAIN ABSOLUTE: *(really annoyed)* For Heaven's
sake, Faulkland, don't expose yourself so. Suppose she
has danced, what then? does not the ceremony of society
often oblige —

FAULKLAND: *(subdued)* Well, well, I'll contain myself
— perhaps, as you say — for form sake. *(to Acres)*
What, Mr. Acres, you were praising Miss Melville's manner of dancing a *minuet* — hey?

ACRES: *(with the confiding frankness of the innocently
unaware)* Oh, I dare insure her for that — but what I
was going to speak of was her *country* dancing: odds
swimmings! she has such an air with her!

FAULKLAND: *(enraged again)* Now disappointment on
her! *(to Captain Absolute)* Defend this, Absolute; why
don't you defend this? Country-dances! jigs and reels!
am I to blame now? A minuet I could have forgiven —
I should not have minded that — *(determined to be absolutely fair and clear about his position)* I say I should

not have regarded a minuet — but country-dances! Zounds! had she made one in a cotillion — I believe I could have forgiven even that — but to be monkey-led for a night! — to run the gauntlet through a string of amorous palming puppies — to show paces like a managed filly! Oh, Jack, there never can be but *one* man in the world, whom a truly modest and delicate woman ought to pair with in a country-dance; and even then the rest of the couples should be her great uncles and aunts!

CAPTAIN ABSOLUTE: *(with heavy sarcasm)* Aye, to be sure! grandfathers and grandmothers!

FAULKLAND: *(racing like a maddened hound down the trail of jealous imaginings)* If there be but one vicious mind in the set, 'twill spread like a contagion — the action of their pulse beats to the lascivious movement of the jig — their quivering, warm-breathed sighs impregnate the very air — the atmosphere becomes electrical to love, and each amorous spark darts through every link of the chain! *(thoroughly upset and aware of the poor figure he has cut in front of a "character" who Captain Absolute had promised would be "diverting")* I must leave you — *(starts toward the door and turns apologetically)* I own I am somewhat flurried — *(in utter anguish as he goes through the door)* — and that confounded looby has perceived it.

CAPTAIN ABSOLUTE: *(calling after him)* Nay, but stay, Faulkland, and thank Mr. Acres for his good news.

FAULKLAND: *(poking his head back in and exiting peremptorily)* Damn his news!

CAPTAIN ABSOLUTE: *(highly amused)* Ha! ha! ha! poor Faulkland five minutes since — "nothing on earth could give him a moment's uneasiness!"

ACRES: *(dimwittedly only half perceiving the implications of what he has said in his enthusiastic praise of Julia)* The gentleman wa'n't angry at my praising his mistress, was he?

CAPTAIN ABSOLUTE: *(sardonically)* A little jealous, I believe, Bob.

ACRES: *(immensely flattered)* You don't say so? Ha! ha! jealous of me — that's a good joke.

CAPTAIN ABSOLUTE: *(with pretended sincerity)* There's nothing strange in that, Bob; let me tell you, that sprightly grace and insinuating manner of yours will do some mischief among the girls here.

ACRES: *(delighted but aware of his previous countrified subservience to his mother and his determination to become a man-about-town at Bath)* Ah! you joke — ha! ha! mischief — ha! ha! but you know I am not my own property, my dear Lydia has forestalled me. She never could abide me in the country, because I used to dress so badly — but odds frogs and tambours! I shan't take matters so here, now ancient madam has no voice in it — I'll make my old clothes know who's master. I shall straightway cashier the hunting-frock, and render my leather breeches incapable. My hair has been in training some time.

CAPTAIN ABSOLUTE: *(with pretended sympathy)* Indeed!

ACRES: Aye — and thoff the side curls are a little restive, my hind-part takes it very kindly.

CAPTAIN ABSOLUTE: *(encouragingly)* Oh, you'll polish, I doubt not.

ACRES: *(buoyantly)* Absolutely I propose so — then if I can find out this Ensign Beverly, odds triggers and flints! I'll make him know the difference o't.

CAPTAIN ABSOLUTE: *(heartily)* Spoke like a man! *(with deferential curiosity)* But pray, Bob, I observe you have got an odd kind of a new method of swearing —

ACRES: *(delighted)* Ha! ha! you've taken notice of it — 'tis genteel, isn't it? — I didn't invent it myself though; but a commander in our militia — a great scholar, I assure you, says that there is no meaning in the common oaths, and that nothing but their antiquity makes them respectable; because, he says, the ancients would never stick to an oath or two, but would say, by Jove! or by Bacchus! or by Mars! or by Venus! or by Pallas! — according to the sentiment — so that to swear with propriety, says my little major, the oath should be an echo to the sense; and we call this the *oath referential,* or *sentimental swearing* — ha! ha! ha! 'tis genteel, isn't it?

CAPTAIN ABSOLUTE: *(with forced gravity)* Very genteel, and very new indeed — and I dare say will supplant all other figures of imprecation.

ACRES: *(profoundly)* Aye, aye, the best terms will grow obsolete. Damns have had their day.

FAG: *(entering to announce another visitor)* Sir, there is a gentleman below who desires to see you. Shall I show him into the parlor?

CAPTAIN ABSOLUTE: Aye, you may.

ACRES: Well, I must be gone —

CAPTAIN ABSOLUTE: *(wondering if the new arrival might provide further amusement at the expense of Acres)* Stay; who is it, Fag?

FAG: *(innocently)* Your father, sir.

CAPTAIN ABSOLUTE: *(heatedly)* You puppy, why didn't you show him up directly? *(Fag bows with a semblance of dignity and exits quickly.)*

ACRES: *(in leave-taking)* You have business with Sir Anthony. I expect a message from Mrs. Malaprop at my lodgings. I have sent also to my dear friend, Sir Lucius O'Trigger. Adieu, Jack, we must meet at night, when you shall give me a dozen bumpers to little Lydia.

CAPTAIN ABSOLUTE: *(cheerfully as Acres departs)* That I will with all my heart. *(alone)* Now for a parental lecture. I hope he has heard nothing of the business that has brought me here. I wish the gout had held him fast in Devonshire, with all my soul! *(turning toward the door to greet his father)* Sir, I am delighted to see you here; and looking so well! your sudden arrival at Bath made me apprehensive for your health.

SIR ANTHONY: *(drily)* Very apprehensive, I dare say, Jack. *(cordially)* What, are you recruiting here, hey?

CAPTAIN ABSOLUTE: Yes, sir, I am on duty.

SIR ANTHONY: Well, Jack, I am glad to see you, though I did not expect it, for I was going to write you on a little matter of business. *(solemnly)* Jack, I have been considering that I grow old and infirm, and shall probably not trouble you long.

CAPTAIN ABSOLUTE: *(in sincere protest)* Pardon me, sir, I never saw you look more strong and hearty; and I pray frequently that you may continue so.

SIR ANTHONY: *(gratified)* I hope your prayers may be heard with all my heart. *(in a businesslike manner)* Well then, Jack, I have been considering that I am so strong and hearty I may continue to plague you a long time. Now, Jack, I am sensible that the income of your commission, and what I have hitherto allowed you, is but a small pittance for a lad of your spirit.

CAPTAIN ABSOLUTE: *(temporizing while trying to take in the implications of this startling announcement)* Sir, you are very good.

SIR ANTHONY: *(broadly)* And it is my wish, while yet I live, to have my boy make some figure in the world. I have resolved, therefore, to fix you at once in a noble independence.

CAPTAIN ABSOLUTE: *(quite taken aback by this unusual display of generosity)* Sir, your kindness overpowers me — such generosity makes the gratitude of reason more lively than the sensations even of filial affection.

SIR ANTHONY: *(broadly)* I am glad you are so sensible of my attention — and you shall be master of a large estate in a few weeks.

CAPTAIN ABSOLUTE: *(with deep feeling)* Let my future life, sir, speak my gratitude: I cannot express the sense I have of your munificence. *(with filial devotion to the wishes of a parent)* Yet, sir, I presume you would not wish me to quit the army?

SIR ANTHONY: *(casually)* Oh, that shall be as your wife chooses.

CAPTAIN ABSOLUTE: *(uncomprehending)* My wife, sir!

SIR ANTHONY: *(waiving this trivial matter aside)* Aye, aye, settle that between you — settle that between you.

CAPTAIN ABSOLUTE: *(puzzled, shocked, and suspicious)* A *wife,* sir, did you say?

SIR ANTHONY: *(offhandedly)* Aye, a wife — why, did not I mention her before?

CAPTAIN ABSOLUTE: *(argumentatively)* Not a word of her, sir.

SIR ANTHONY: Odd so! — I mustn't forget *her,* though. *(as if explaining the obvious)* Yes, Jack, the independence I was talking of is by marriage — the fortune is saddled with a wife — *(airily)* — but I suppose that makes no difference.

CAPTAIN ABSOLUTE: *(stunned)* Sir! sir! — you amaze me!

SIR ANTHONY: *(lightheartedly but with just a trace of anger)* Why, what the devil's the matter with the fool? Just now you were all gratitude and duty.

CAPTAIN ABSOLUTE: *(reasonably)* I was sir — you talked to me of independence and a fortune, but not a word of a wife.

SIR ANTHONY: *(as if amazed at his son's lack of worldly knowledge)* Why, what difference does that make? Odds life, sir! if you have the estate, you must take it with the live stock on it, as it stands.

CAPTAIN ABSOLUTE: *(stiffly)* If my happiness is to be the price, I must beg leave to decline the purchase. *(curiously)* Pray, sir, who is the lady?

SIR ANTHONY: *(as if the question were preposterous)* What's that to you, sir? *(with genial persuasion)* Come, give me your promise to love and marry her directly.

CAPTAIN ABSOLUTE: *(appealing to his father's sense of justice)* Sure, sir, this is not very reasonable, to summon my affections for a lady I know nothing of!

SIR ANTHONY: *(with serene confidence in his authority)* I am sure, sir, 'tis more unreasonable in you to *object* to a lady you know nothing of.

CAPTAIN ABSOLUTE: *(quietly but firmly)* Then, sir, I must tell you plainly, that my inclinations are fixed on another — my heart is engaged to an angel.

SIR ANTHONY: *(amused at this innocent prattle)* Then pray let it send an excuse. It is very sorry — but *business* prevents its waiting on her.

CAPTAIN ABSOLUTE: *(ignoring his father's cleverness)* But my vows are pledged to her.

SIR ANTHONY: *(tartly)* Let her foreclose, Jack; let her foreclose; they are not worth redeeming; besides, you have the angel's vows in exchange, I suppose; so there can be no loss there.

CAPTAIN ABSOLUTE: *(unimpressed with this self-willed cynical sophistry)* You must excuse me, sir, if I tell you, once for all, that in this point I cannot obey you.

SIR ANTHONY: *(sternly)* Hark'ee, Jack; — I have heard you for some time with patience. *(his temper rising)* I have been cool — quite cool; but take care — you know I am compliance itself — when I am not thwarted; no one more easily led — when I have my own way; — but don't put me in a frenzy.

CAPTAIN ABSOLUTE: *(quietly)* Sir, I must repeat it — in this I cannot obey you.

SIR ANTHONY: *(not really convinced of his son's intransigence, incapable of understanding anything opposed to his own wishes, and expecting to end opposition by a threat of disinheritance)* Now damn me! if ever I call you *Jack* again while I live!

CAPTAIN ABSOLUTE: *(appealingly)* Nay, sir, but hear me.

SIR ANTHONY: *(with good-natured severity and confidently expecting his son's compliance)* Sir, I won't hear a word — not a word! not one word! so give me your promise with a nod — *(persuasively)* — and I'll tell you what, Jack — *(affectionately)* — I mean, you dog — if you don't, by —

CAPTAIN ABSOLUTE: *(interrupting and raising his voice in protest)* What, sir, promise to link myself to some mass of ugliness! to —

SIR ANTHONY: *(drowning out his son with the rage of the obstructed tyrant)* Zounds! sirrah! the lady shall be as ugly as I choose: she shall have a hump on each shoulder; she shall be as crooked as the crescent; her one eye shall roll like the bull in Cox's Museum; she shall have a skin like a mummy, and the beard of a Jew — she shall be all this, sirrah! yet I'll make you ogle her all day, and sit up all night to write sonnets on her beauty.

CAPTAIN ABSOLUTE: *(appalled)* This is reason and moderation indeed!

SIR ANTHONY: *(angrily)* None of your sneering, puppy! no grinning, jackanapes!

CAPTAIN ABSOLUTE: *(gloomily)* Indeed, sir, I never was in a worse humor for mirth in my life.

SIR ANTHONY: *(now convinced that whatever is, is wrong)* 'Tis false, sir! I know you are laughing in your sleeve; I know you'll grin when I am gone, sirrah!

CAPTAIN ABSOLUTE: *(humbly)* Sir, I hope I know my duty better.

SIR ANTHONY: *(in a loud domineering voice)* None of your passion, sir! none of your violence, if you please!
—It won't do with me, I promise you.

CAPTAIN ABSOLUTE: *(matter-of-factly)* Indeed, sir, I never was cooler in my life.

SIR ANTHONY: *(shouting)* 'Tis a confounded lie! — I know you are in a passion in your heart; I know you are, you hypocritical young dog! but it won't do.

CAPTAIN ABSOLUTE: *(placatingly)* Nay, sir, upon my word —

SIR ANTHONY: *(in the height of outraged passion)* So, you will fly out! can't you be cool, like me? What the devil good can passion do? — Passion is of no service, you impudent, insolent, overbearing reprobate! *(Captain Absolute winces.)* There, you sneer again! don't provoke me! — but you rely upon the mildness of my temper — you do, you dog! you play upon the meekness of my disposition! — Yet take care — the patience of a saint may be overcome at last! — but mark! *(subduing his voice to a tone of cold precision)* I give you six hours and a half to consider of this: if you then agree, without any condition, to do everything on earth I choose, *(ameliorating)* why — confound you! I may in time forgive you. — If not, zounds! don't enter the same hemisphere with me! *(his voice rising again in a steady crescendo)* don't dare to breathe the same air, or use the same light with me;

but get an atmosphere and a sun of your own! I'll strip you of your commission; I'll lodge a five-and-threepence in the hands of trustees, and you shall live on the interest. *(with climactic vehemence)* I'll disown you, I'll disinherit you, I'll unget you! and damn me, if ever I call you Jack again! *(He slams out of the room.)*

CAPTAIN ABSOLUTE: *(looking after him)* Mild, gentle, considerate father — I kiss your hands! — What a tender method of giving his opinion in these matters Sir Anthony has! I dare not trust him with the truth. *(musing)* I wonder what old wealthy hag it is that he wants to bestow on me! — Yet he married himself for love! and was in his youth a bold intriguer, and a gay companion! *(He is interrupted by the entrance of Fag.)*

FAG: *(with an expression of supercilious amusement)* Assuredly, sir, your father is wrath to a degree; he comes down stairs eight or ten steps at a time — muttering, growling, and thumping the bannisters all the way: I and the cook's dog stand bowing at the door — rap! he gives me a stroke on the head with his cane; bids me carry *that* to my master; then kicking the poor turnspit[4] into the area, damns us all, for a puppy triumvirate! *(showing complete disrespect for Sir Anthony)* Upon my credit, sir, were I in your place, and found my father such very bad company, I should certainly drop his acquaintance.

CAPTAIN ABSOLUTE: *(sounding exactly like his father)* Cease your impertinence, sir, at present. Did you come in for nothing more? — Stand out of the way! *(pushes Fag roughly aside and, without realizing it, imitates his father's exit.)*

FAG: *(soliloquizing much as his master has just done after his father's departure)* Soh! Sir Anthony trims my master; he is afraid to reply to his father — then vents his spleen on poor Fag! When one is vexed by one person, to revenge one's self on another, who happens to come in the way, is the vilest injustice! Ah! it shows the

---

[4] A breed of dog, much like a dachsund.

worst temper — the basest — *(He is interrupted by the entrance of an errand boy.)*

BOY: Mr. Fag! Mr. Fag! your master calls you.

FAG: *(contemptuously)* Well, you little dirty puppy, you need not bawl so! *(resuming his musing)* — The meanest disposition! the —

BOY: *(urgently)* Quick, quick, Mr. Fag!

FAG: *(shouting in exact imitation of Captain Absolute)* Quick! quick! you impudent jackanapes! am I to be commanded by you too? *(kicking him out of the door)* you little impertinent, insolent, kitchen-bred — *(The remainder of this string of opprobrious epithets is lost to the audience because Fag rages out after the boy, completing a trio of identical exits.)*

Scene Two

The North Parade, a broad paved walk, free from mud, traffic, and the vulgar; located near the Pump Room, the Roman Baths, and the handsome Assembly Rooms. The row of austerely simple stone houses lining one side is viewed by the audience. (On the other side, open country slopes down and away from the promenade.) As the scene opens, Lucy saunters on from the right. She pauses and looks around as if expecting to meet someone.

LUCY: *(ruminating over the visit of Sir Anthony to Mrs. Malaprop)* So — I shall have another rival to add to my mistress's list — Captain Absolute. However, I shall not enter his name till my purse has received notice in form. Poor Acres is dismissed! Well, I have done him a last friendly office in letting him know that Beverley was here before him. *(with a trace of annoyance at being kept waiting)* Sir Lucius is generally more punctual when he expects to hear from his *dear Dalia,* as he calls her: I wonder he's not here! *(pensively)* I have a little scruple of conscience from this deceit; though I should not be paid so well if my hero knew that *Delia* was near fifty, and her own mistress.

Sir Lucius O'Trigger enters from the right. He is unusually tall and, in spite of his advancing years, he presents a striking appearance: his jaunty cocked hat, dark blue dress coat with gilt buttons, white waistcoat and ruffled shirt are set off by black breeches, silk stockings, and buckled shoes. He is an infatuated fanatic of duelling, an Indian-summer romanticist — chivalry on the verge of senility. His face lights up as he spies Lucy waiting for him. He steps briskly up to her and speaks with a pronounced brogue as indicated by her reference to his pronunciation of Delia.

SIR LUCIUS: Ha! my little ambassadress — upon my conscience, I have been looking for you; I have been on the South Parade this half hour.

LUCY: *(with affected simplicity)* O gemini! and I have been waiting for your worship here on the North.

SIR LUCIUS: *(with heavy Irish accent and manner)* Faith! — maybe that was the reason we did not meet; *(with light sarcasm)* and it is very comical too, how you could go out and I not see you — *(humorously to excuse her apparent lie of having waited long for him)* for I was only taking a nap at the Parade Coffee-house, and I chose the window on purpose that I might not miss you.

LUCY: *(with deliberate simple-minded earnestness)* My stars! Now I'd wager a sixpence I went by while you were asleep.

SIR LUCIUS: *(good-naturedly)* Sure enough it must have been so — and I never dreamt it was so late, till I waked. Well, but my little girl, have you got nothing for me?

LUCY: *(simpering)* Yes, but I have — I've got a letter for you in my pocket.

SIR LUCIUS: *(brightening)* O faith! I guessed you weren't come empty-handed. Well — let me see what the dear creature says.

LUCY: *(demurely as she hands him a letter)* There, Sir Lucius.

SIR LUCIUS: *(opening it quickly and reading slowly*

and with apparent difficulty) "Sir — there is often a sudden impulse in love, that has a greater induction[1] than years of domestic combination:[2] such was the commotion[3] I felt at the first superfluous[4] view of Sir Lucius O'Trigger." *(raising his eyes and commenting, to Lucy)* Very pretty, upon my word. *(resuming his reading)* "Female punctuation[5] forbids me to say more; yet let me add, that it will give me joy infallible[6] to find Sir Lucius worthy the last criterion[7] of my affections. Delia." *(to Lucy)* Upon my conscience! Lucy, your lady is a great mistress of language. *(in recognition of the malapropisms)* Faith, she's quite the queen of the dictionary! — for the devil a word dare refuse coming at her call — though one would think it was quite out of hearing.

LUCY: *(momentarily forgetting that she has been representing Lydia, not Mrs. Malaprop, as the writer of these billets-doux)* Aye, sir, a lady of her experience —

SIR LUCIUS: Experience! what, at seventeen?

LUCY: *(recovering)* O true, sir — but then she reads so — my stars! how she will read offhand!

SIR LUCIUS: *(interested)* Faith, she must be very deep read to write this way — though she is rather an arbitrary writer too — for here are a great many poor words pressed into the service of this note, that would get their *habeas corpus* from any court in Christendom.[8]

LUCY: *(assuming that his incomprehensible comment was unadulterated praise, and intent on her private bus-*

---

[1] Did she mean *seduction?*

[2] *Cohabitation?*

[3] *Emotion?*

[4] *Superficial.*

[5] *Punctiliousness* or *punctilio.*

[6] *Ineffable.*

[7] She seems to have meant "the last *degree, iota, scintilla,*" but what word did she have in mind?

[8] An elaborate image which implies that the letter-writer has acted as a tryant in forcing words to perform services not usually required of them and that, under English law, she could be required to produce them in court in answer to charges that she was putting illegal restraints upon their freedom.

iness of fanning his ardor) Ah! Sir Lucius, if you were to hear how she talks of you!

SIR LUCIUS: *(in hearty eagerness to win this young girl whose wealth and beauty easily compensate for her verbal peccadillos)* Oh, tell her I'll make her the best husband in the world, and Lady O'Trigger into the bargain! *(in recognition that Lucy might be tempted to resort to unscrupulous devices in pursuit of her own interests)* But we must get the old gentlewoman's consent — and do everything fairly.

LUCY: *(coyly)* Nay, Sir Lucius, I thought you wa'n't rich enough to be so nice!

SIR LUCIUS: *(laughing)* Upon my word, young woman, you have hit it: — I am so poor that I can't afford to do a dirty action. If I did not want money, I'd steal your mistress and her fortune with a great deal of pleasure. However, my pretty girl, *(reaching in his pocket for a tip which he gives her)* here's a little something to buy you a ribbon; and meet me in the evening, and I'll give you an answer to this. *(with offhanded self-confidence)* So, hussy, take a kiss beforehand to put you in mind. *(He kisses her.)*

LUCY: *(archly)* O Lud! Sir Lucius — I never seed such a gemman! My lady won't like you if you're so impudent.

SIR LUCIUS: *(in high good-humor)* Faith she will, Lucy! That same — pho! what's the name of it? — modesty — is a quality in a lover more praised by the women than liked; so, if your mistress asks you whether Sir Lucius ever gave you a kiss, tell her *fifty* — my dear.

LUCY: *(flirtatiously)* What, would you have me tell a lie?

SIR LUCIUS: *(putting his arm about her waist and pulling her toward him)* Ah, then, you baggage! I'll make it a truth presently.

LUCY: *(abruptly pulling away as she suddenly realizes that they are being observed)* For shame now! here is some one coming.

SIR LUCIUS: *(not at all disturbed but sympathetic)*

Oh, faith, I'll quiet your conscience. *(He bows formally as if to a lady and saunters off stage to the right, humming a tune.)*

FAG: *(entering from the left and behaving with the greatest civility)* So, so, ma'am! I humbly beg pardon.

LUCY: *(giggling)* O Lud, now, Mr. Fag — you flurry one so.

FAG: *(with a superior manner)* Come, come, Lucy, here's no one by — so a little less simplicity, with a grain or two more sincerity, if you please. You play false with us, madam. I saw you give the baronet a letter. *(dramatically)* My master shall know this — and if he don't call him out, I will.

LUCY: *(unimpressed)* Ha! ha! ha! you gentlemen's gentlemen are so hasty. That letter was from Mrs. Malaprop, simpleton. She is taken with Sir Lucius's address.

FAG: *(pretending to be affronted)* How! what tastes some people have! Why, I suppose *I* have walked by her window a hundred times! *(back to business)* But what says our young lady? any message to my master?

LUCY: *(morosely)* Sad news, Mr. Fag. A worse rival than Acres! Sir Anthony Absolute has proposed his son.

FAG: *(tentatively)* What, Captain Absolute?

LUCY: *(insistently)* Even so — I overheard it all.

FAG: *(delighted with his secret knowledge)* Ha! ha! ha! very good, faith. Good-bye, Lucy, I must away with this news.

LUCY: *(provoked)* Well, you may laugh — but it is true, I assure you. *(making as if to leave and proffering a note of hope)* But, Mr. Fag, tell your master not to be cast down by this.

FAG: *(with mock seriousness)* Oh, he'll be so disconsolate!

LUCY: *(moving toward the right wings)* And charge him not to think of quarrelling with young Absolute.

FAG: *(starting to exit to left and calling out cheerfully)* Never fear! never fear!

LUCY: *(exiting to right)* — bid him keep up his spirits.

FAG: *(exiting to left)* We will — we will.

ACT THREE

Scene One

The same. The North Parade. Captain Absolute enters from the left proceeding in the general direction of his father's lodgings, having been informed by Fag who his intended wife actually is.

CAPTAIN ABSOLUTE: 'Tis just as Fag told me, indeed. Whimsical enough, faith! My father wants to force me to marry the very girl I am plotting to run away with! He must not know of my connection with her yet awhile. He has too summary a method of proceeding in these matters. However, I'll read my recantation instantly. My conversion is something sudden, indeed — but I can assure him it is very *sincere. (suddenly observing that his father is approaching from the right)* So, so — here he comes. He looks plaguy gruff. *(retreating to the shadows in the back of the stage)*

SIR ANTHONY: *(entering from the right and muttering to himself)* No — I'll die sooner than forgive him. Die, did I say? I'll live these fifty years to plague him. At our last meeting, his impudence had almost put me out of temper. An obstinate, passionate, self-willed boy! Who can he take after? This is my reward for getting him before all his brothers and sisters! — for putting him, at twelve years old, into a marching regiment, and allowing him fifty pounds a year, besides his pay, ever since! *(gloomily)* I never will see him more, never — never — never — never.

CAPTAIN ABSOLUTE: *(to himself)* Now for a penitential face. *(walking forward directly into his father's path)*

SIR ANTHONY: *(pretending non-recognition)* Fellow, get out of my way!

CAPTAIN ABSOLUTE: *(with deep humility)* Sir, you see a penitent before you.

SIR ANTHONY: *(pretending anger but secretly pleased)* I see an impudent scoundrel before me.

CAPTAIN ABSOLUTE: *(plaintively)* A sincere penitent. I am come, sir, to acknowledge my error, and to submit entirely to your will.

SIR ANTHONY: *(utterly amazed and inwardly delighted)* What's that?

CAPTAIN ABSOLUTE: *(humbly)* I have been revolving, and reflecting, and considering on your past goodness, and kindness, and condescension to me.

SIR ANTHONY: *(tentatively)* Well, sir?

CAPTAIN ABSOLUTE: *(in a melting tone)* I have been likewise weighing and balancing what you were pleased to mention concerning duty, and obedience, and authority.

SIR ANTHONY: *(affectionately though with an appearance of gruffness)* Well, puppy?

CAPTAIN ABSOLUTE: *(with self-conscious nobility)* Why then, sir, the result of my reflection is — a resolution to sacrifice every inclination of my own to your satisfaction.

SIR ANTHONY: *(enormously pleased)* Why now you talk sense — absolute sense — I never heard anything more sensible in my life. *(expansively)* Confound you! you shall be Jack again.

CAPTAIN ABSOLUTE: *(meekly)* I shall be happy in the appellation.

SIR ANTHONY: *(with heartfelt good-will)* Why, then, Jack, my dear Jack, I will now inform you who the lady really is. Nothing but your passion and violence, you silly fellow, prevented my telling you at first. *(dramatically)* Prepare, Jack, for wonder and rapture — prepare. *(in a deliberately offhand conversational tone)* What think you of Miss Lydia Languish?

CAPTAIN ABSOLUTE: *(pretending utter ignorance and some puzzlement)* Languish! What, the Languishes of Worcestershire?

SIR ANTHONY: *(amused)* Worcestershire! No. Did you never meet Mrs. Malaprop and her niece, Miss Languish, who came into our country just before you were last ordered to your regiment?

CAPTAIN ABSOLUTE: *(as if groping in his memory)* Malaprop! Languish! I don't remember ever to have heard the names before. *(with sudden pretended remembrance)* Yet, stay — I think I do recollect something. *Languish! Languish!* She squints, don't she? A little red-haired girl?

SIR ANTHONY: *(with complete innocence)* Squints? A red-haired girl! Zounds! no.

CAPTAIN ABSOLUTE: *(just as innocently)* Then I must have forgot; it can't be the same person.

SIR ANTHONY: *(mellowing)* Jack! Jack! what think you of blooming, love-breathing seventeen.

CAPTAIN ABSOLUTE: *(dutifully)* As to that, sir, I am quite indifferent. If I can please you in the matter, 'tis all I desire.

SIR ANTHONY: *(rapturously)* Nay, but Jack, such eyes! such eyes! so innocently wild! so bashfully irresolute! not a glance but speaks and kindles some thought of love! Then, Jack, her cheeks! her cheeks, Jack! so deeply blushing at the insinuation of her tell-tale eyes! Then, Jack, her lips! O Jack, lips smiling at their own discretion; and if not smiling, more sweetly pouting; more lovely in sullenness!

CAPTAIN ABSOLUTE: *(aside to audience)* That's she, indeed. Well done, old gentleman.

SIR ANTHONY: *(quite carried away by this theme)* Then, Jack, her neck! O Jack! Jack!

CAPTAIN ABSOLUTE: *(with painful matter-of-factness)* And which is to be mine, sir, the niece, or the aunt?

SIR ANTHONY: *(baffled and outraged)* Why, you unfeeling, insensible puppy, I despise you. When I was of your age, such a description would have made me fly like a rocket! The *aunt* indeed! Odds life! when I ran away with your mother, I would not have touched anything old or ugly to gain an empire.

CAPTAIN ABSOLUTE: *(gently)* Not to please your father, sir?

SIR ANTHONY: To please my father! Zounds! not to please — *(recollecting himself)* Oh, my father — odd so! — yes — yes; if my father indeed had desired — that's quite another matter. Though he wa'n't the indulgent father that I am, Jack.

CAPTAIN ABSOLUTE: *(earnestly)* I dare say not, sir.

SIR ANTHONY: *(completely nonplussed)* But, Jack, you are not sorry to find your mistress is so beautiful?

CAPTAIN ABSOLUTE: *(like a schoolboy reciting a lesson by rote)* Sir, I repeat it; if I please you in this affair, 'tis all I desire. Not that I think a woman the worse for being handsome; but, sir, if you please to recollect, you before hinted something about a hump or two, one eye, and a few more graces of that kind — now, without being very nice, I own I should rather choose a wife of mine to have the usual number of limbs, and a limited quantity of back: and though one eye may be very agreeable, yet as the prejudice has always run in favor of two, I would not wish to effect a singularity in that article.

SIR ANTHONY: *(in horror)* What a phlegmatic sot it is! Why, sirrah, you're an anchorite! — a vile, insensible stock. You a soldier! — you're a walking block, fit only to dust the company's regimentals on! *(exclaiming)* Odds life! I've a great mind to marry the girl myself!

CAPTAIN ABSOLUTE: *(obediently)* I am entirely at your disposal, sir: if you should think of addressing Miss Languish yourself, I suppose you would have me marry the aunt; or if you should change your mind, and take the old lady — 'tis the same to me — I'll marry the niece.

SIR ANTHONY: *(exhausted)* Upon my word, Jack, thou'rt either a very great hypocrite, or — *(half-understanding and indulgently pleased with his son's play-acting)* But come, I know your indifference on such a subject must be all a lie — I'm sure it must — come, now — damn your demure face! — come, confess Jack — you have been lying — ha'n't you? You have been playing the hypocrite, hey! — I'll never forgive you, if you ha'n't been lying and playing the hypocrite.

CAPTAIN ABSOLUTE: *(with no retreat from his pose)* I'm sorry, sir, that the respect and duty which I bear to you should be so mistaken.

SIR ANTHONY: *(vehemently)* Hang your respect and duty! *(affectionately)* But come along with me, I'll write a note to Mrs. Malaprop, and you shall visit the lady directly. Her eyes shall be the Promethean torch to you — come along, I'll never forgive you if you don't come back stark mad with rapture and impatience — *(humorously)* If you don't, egad, I'll marry the girl myself! *(They go off together.)*

Scene Two

Julia's Dressing Room in the lodgings rented by Sir Anthony. Much like Lydia's room, it contains a dressing table and a few casual chairs, a dresser, and a sofa. As the scene opens Faulkland is nervously pacing up and down. He has been admitted awhile back and is awaiting Julia's return to her apartment.

FAULKLAND: *(in fretful self-analysis)* They told me Julia would return directly; I wonder she is not yet come! How mean does this captious, unsatisfied temper of mine appear to my cooler judgment! Yet I know not that I indulge it in any other point: but on this one subject, and to this one object, whom I think I love beyond my life, I am ever ungenerously fretful and madly capricious! I am conscious of it — yet I cannot correct myself! *(in a glow of reminiscense)* What tender, honest joy sparkled in her eyes when we met! How delicate was the warmth of her expressions! I was ashamed to appear less happy — though I had come resolved to wear a face of coolness and upbraiding. Sir Anthony's presence prevented my proposed expostulations; yet I must be satisfied that she has not been so *very* happy in my absence. *(listening)*

She is coming! Yes! I know the nimbleness of her tread, when she thinks her impatient Faulkland counts the moments of her stay.

JULIA: *(entering and radiating spontaneous pleasure at seeing Faulkland)* I had not hoped to see you again so soon.

FAULKLAND: *(a trifle stiffly)* Could I, Julia, be contented with my first welcome — restrained as we were by the presence of a third person?

JULIA: *(affectionately)* O Faulkland, when your kindness can make me thus happy, let me not think that I discovered something of coldness in your first salutation.

FAULKLAND: *(not thawing)* 'Twas but your fancy, Julia. I was rejoiced to see you — *(insinuatingly)* — to see you in such health. Sure I had no cause for coldness?

JULIA: *(openly)* Nay, then, I see you have taken something ill. You must not conceal from me what it is.

FAULKLAND: *(querulously)* Well, then — shall I own to you that my joy at hearing of your health and arrival here, by your neighbor Acres, was somewhat damped by his dwelling much on the high spirits you had enjoyed in Devonshire — on your mirth — your singing — dancing, and I know not what? For such is my temper, Julia, that I should regard every mirthful moment in your absence as a treason to constancy: the mutual tear that steals down the cheek of parting lovers is a compact that no smile shall live there till they meet again.

JULIA: *(in a kindly tone but with a trace of impatience)* Must I never cease to tax my Faulkland with this teasing minute caprice? Can the idle reports of a silly boor weigh in your breast against my tried affection?

FAULKLAND: *(persisting in his self-torture)* They have no weight with me, Julia: no, no — I am happy if you have been so — yet only say, that you did not sing with *mirth* — say that you *thought* of Faulkland in the dance.

JULIA: *(with forthright honesty)* I never can be happy in your absence. If I wear a countenance of content, it is to show that my mind holds no doubt of my Faulkland's truth. If I seemed sad, it were to make malice triumph:

*The contract which my poor father bound us in
gives you more than a lover's privilege.*

and say that I had fixed my heart on one who left me to lament his roving and my own credulity. *(earnestly)* Believe me, Faulkland, I mean not to upbraid you when I say that I have often dressed sorrow in smiles, lest my friends should guess whose unkindness had caused my tears.

FAULKLAND: *(overcome)* You were ever all goodness to me. Oh, I am a brute, when I but admit a doubt of your true constancy!

JULIA: *(gravely)* If ever, without such cause from you, as I will not suppose possible, you find my affections veering but a point, may I become a proverbial scoff for levity and base ingratitude.

FAULKLAND: *(rebukingly)* Ah! Julia, that last word is grating to me. I would I had no title to your *gratitude!* Search your heart, Julia; perhaps what you have mistaken for love is but the warm effusion of a too thankful heart.

JULIA: *(puzzled)* For what quality must I love you?

FAULKLAND: *(perversely)* For no quality! To regard me for any quality of mind or understanding were only to *esteem* me. And for person — I have often wished myself deformed, to be convinced that I owed no obligation *there* for any part of your affection.

JULIA: *(agreeably but with her usual complete candor)* Where nature has bestowed a show of nice attention in the features of a man, he should laugh at it, as misplaced. I *have* seen men, who in this vain article, perhaps, might rank above you; but my heart has never asked my eyes if it were so or not.

FAULKLAND: *(discovering a new cause for grief)* Now this is not well from *you,* Julia — I despise person in a man — yet, if you loved me as I wish, though I were an Aethiop, you'd think none so fair.

JULIA: *(at the end of her patience)* I see you are determined to be unkind. The *contract* which my poor father bound us in gives you more than a lover's privilege.

FAULKLAND: *(miserably)* Again, Julia, you raise ideas that feed and justify my doubts. I would not have been more free — no — I am proud of my restraint. Yet — yet — perhaps your high respect alone for this solemn compact has fettered your inclinations, which else had made a worthier choice. How shall I be sure, had you remained unbound in thought and promise, that I could still have been the object of your persevering love?

JULIA: *(bluntly)* Then try me now. Let us be free as strangers as to what is past: *my* heart will not feel more liberty!

FAULKLAND: *(determined to fix a wrong meaning even on this candid statement of her devotion)* There now! so hasty, Julia! so anxious to be free! If your love for me were fixed and ardent, you would not lose your hold, even though I wished it!

JULIA: *(on the verge of tears)* Oh! you torture me to the heart! I cannot bear it.

FAULKLAND: *(with almost psychopathic persistence in examining the motive)* I do not mean to distress you. If I loved you less, I should never give you an uneasy moment. But hear me. All my fretful doubts arise from this. Women are not used to weigh, and separate the motives of their affections: the cold dictates of prudence, gratitude, or filial duty, may sometimes be mistaken for the pleadings of the heart. I would not boast — yet let me say, that I have neither age, person, nor character to found dislike on; my fortune, such as few ladies could be charged with indiscretion in the match. O Julia! when *Love* receives such countenance from *Prudence,* nice minds will be suspicious of its birth.

JULIA: *(in anguished tones)* I know not whither your insinuations would tend: but as they seem pressing to insult me, I will spare you the regret of having done so. *(bursting into tears and rushing from the room)* I have given you no cause for this!

FAULKLAND: *(alone and somewhat bewildered by the effect of his "reasonable" discourse)* In tears! *(calling as he goes to the door at the right which she has just slammed behind her)* Stay, Julia: stay but for a moment. *(putting his hand on the door knob as if to follow her)* The door is fastened! *(calling)* Julia! my soul! — but for one moment! *(listening)* I hear her sobbing! *(in angry self-accusation)* 'Sdeath! what a brute am I to use her thus! *(listening)* Yet stay. Aye, she is coming now. *(smugly perverse)* How little resolution there is in woman! how a few soft words can turn them! *(pausing expectantly)* No, faith! she is *not* coming either. *(calling again in a honeyed tone)* Why, Julia — my love — say but that you forgive me — come but to tell me that. *(annoyed)* Now this is being *too* resentful. *(listening again)* Stay! she *is* coming too. *(with a smile of semi-lunatic superiority)* I thought she would — no steadiness in anything! Her going away must have been a mere trick then — she sha'n't see that I was hurt by it. I'll affect indifference. *(hums a tune to himself)* No — zounds! she's not coming! — nor don't intend it, I suppose. *(angrily)* This is not steadiness, but obstinancy! *(miserably)* Yet I deserve it. What, after so long an absence to quarrel with her tenderness! — 'twas barbarous and unmanly! I should be ashamed to see her now. — I'll wait till her just resentment is abated — and *(dramatically)* when I distress her so again, may I lose her forever, and be linked instead to some antique virago, whose gnawing passions, and long-hoarded spleen, shall make me curse my folly half the day and all the night! *(He stalks offstage to the left in self-accusing remorsefulness, as dissatisfied now with himself as he was originally with Julia.)*

Scene Three

The drawing room at Mrs. Malaprop's lodgings. It is quite elaborately furnished though giving the impression of expensive rented quarters rather than anyone's home. Mrs. Malaprop is holding a letter in her hand, and discoursing elegantly with the bearer of the letter, Captain Absolute. This is, of course, the note which Sir Anthony promised his son in the preceding scene as an introduction to "the aunt and the niece."

MRS. MALAPROP: *(graciously)* Your being Sir Anthony's son, captain, would itself be a sufficient accomodation;[1] but from the ingenuity[2] of your appearance, I am convinced you deserve the character here given of you.

CAPTAIN ABSOLUTE: *(with broad flattery)* Permit me to say, madam, that as I never yet have had the pleasure of seeing Miss Languish, my principal inducement in this affair at present is the honor of being allied to Mrs. Malaprop; of whose intellectual accomplishments, elegant manners, and unaffected learning, no tongue is silent.

MRS. MALAPROP: *(obviously pleased that justice has been done to her accomplishments)* Sir, you do me infinite honor! I beg, Captain, you'll be seated. *(gracefully indicating a chair. He bows deeply as she relaxes into the chair beside it, and then sits down herself.)* Ah! few gentlemen, nowadays, know how to value the ineffectual[3] qualities in a woman! few think how a little knowledge becomes a gentlewoman! Men have no sense now but for the worthless flower of beauty!

CAPTAIN ABSOLUTE: *(with simulated sympathy)* It is but too true indeed, ma'am; yet I feel our ladies should share the blame — they think our admiration of beauty so great, that knowledge in them would be superfluous. *(launching into an eloquent figure)* Thus, like garden trees, they seldom show fruit, till time has robbed them of the more specious blossoms. Few, like Mrs. Malaprop and the orange-tree, are rich in both at once!

MRS. MALAPROP: *(accepting this gross flattery at its face value)* Sir, you overpower me with good-breeding. *(as if addressing the world)* He is the very pineapple[4] of politeness. *(confidentially to Captain Absolute)* You are not ignorant, Captain, that this giddy girl has somehow contrived to fix her affections on a beggarly, strolling, eaves-dropping ensign, whom none of us have seen, and nobody knows anything of?

---

[1] *Recommendation.*

[2] *Ingenuousness?*

[3] *Intellectual.*

[4] *Pinnacle.*

CAPTAIN ABSOLUTE: *(easily)* Oh, I have heard the silly affair before. I'm not at all prejudiced against her on *that* account.

MRS. MALAPROP: *(earnestly)* You are very good and very considerate, Captain. I am sure I have done everything in my power since I exploded[5] the affair; long ago I laid my positive conjunctions[6] on her, never to think on the fellow again; I have since laid Sir Anthony's preposition[7] before her; but, I am sorry to say, she seems resolved to decline every particle[8] that I enjoin her.

CAPTAIN ABSOLUTE: *(pretending deep concern)* It must be very distressing, indeed, ma'am.

MRS. MALAPROP:*(with a great sigh)* Oh! it gives me the hydrostatics[9] to such a degree. I thought she had persisted[10] from corresponding with him; but, behold, this very day I have interceded[11] another letter from the fellow; I believe I have it in my pocked. *(fishing for it)*

CAPTAIN ABSOLUTE: *(aside)* Oh, the devil! my last note.

MRS. MALAPROP: *(pulling it out)* Aye, here it is.

CAPTAIN ABSOLUTE: *(recognizing it — aside)* Aye, my note indeed! Oh, the little traitress Lucy.

MRS. MALAPROP: *(handing him the letter)* There, perhaps you may know the writing.

CAPTAIN ABSOLUTE: *(peering at it intently)* I think I have seen the hand before — yes, I certainly must have seen this hand before —

MRS. MALAPROP: Nay, but read it, captain.

CAPTAIN ABSOLUTE: *(reading)* "My soul's idol, my adored Lydia;" *(looking up)* Very tender indeed!

MRS. MALAPROP: *(vehemently)* Tender! aye, and profane too, o' my conscience!

---

6 *Exposed?*

6 *Injunctions.*

7 *Proposition.*

8 *Article.*

9 *Hysterics?*

10 *Desisted.*

11 *Intercepted.*

CAPTAIN ABSOLUTE: *(returning to his reading)* "I am excessively alarmed at the intelligence you send me, the more so as my new rival —"

MRS. MALAPROP: *(interrupting)* That's *you,* sir.

CAPTAIN ABSOLUTE: "Has universally the character of being an accomplished gentleman, and a man of honor —" *(pausing with pleasure at his own account of himself)* Well, that's handsome enough.

MRS. MALAPROP: *(deprecatingly)* Oh, the fellow has some design in writing so.

CAPTAIN ABSOLUTE: *(emphatically)* That he had, I'll answer for him, ma'am.

MRS. MALAPROP: But go on, sir — you'll see presently.

CAPTAIN ABSOLUTE: *(reading with some hesitation)* "As for the old weather-beaten she-dragon who guards you —" *(looking up in innocent amazement)* Who can he mean by that?

MRS. MALAPROP: *(outraged)* Me, sir! *me* — he means me! There — what do you think now? — but go on a little further.

CAPTAIN ABSOLUTE: *(pretending to share her disgust)* Impudent scoundrel! *(resuming his reading)* "— it shall go hard but I will elude her vigilance, as I am told that the same ridiculous vanity, which makes her dress up her coarse features, and deck her dull chat with hard words which she don't understand —"

MRS. MALAPROP: *(interrupting)* There, sir, an attack upon my language! what do you think of that? — an aspersion upon my parts of speech! Was ever such a brute! Sure, if I reprehend[12] anything in this world, it is the use of my oracular[13] tongue, and a nice derangement of epitaphs![14]

CAPTAIN ABSOLUTE: *(indignantly)* He deserves to be hanged and quartered! *(returning to the note)* Let me see — "same ridiculous vanity —"

---

[12] *Comprehend.*

[13] *Vernacular?*

[14] *Arrangement of epithets.*

MRS. MALAPROP: *(touchily)* You need not read it again, sir.

CAPTAIN ABSOLUTE: *(humbly)* I beg pardon, ma'am. *(continues)* "— does also lay her open to the grossest deceptions from flattery and pretended admiration —" *(exclaiming)* An impudent coxcomb! *(resuming)* "— so that I have a scheme to see you shortly with the old harridan's consent, and even to make her a go-between in our interview." *(looking up in amazement)* Was ever such assurance!

MRS. MALAPROP: Did you ever hear anything like it? — he'll elude my vigilance, will he? — yes, yes, ha! ha! *(ironically)* He's *very* likely to enter these doors! — we'll try who can plot best!

CAPTAIN ABSOLUTE: *(enthusiastically)* So we will, ma'am — so we will. Ha! ha! ha! a conceited puppy, ha! ha! ha! Well, but, Mrs. Malaprop, as the girl seems so infatuated by this fellow, suppose you were to wink at her corresponding with him for a little time — let her even plot an elopement with him — then do you connive at her escape — while *I,* just in the nick, will have the fellow laid by the heels, and fairly connive to carry her off in his stead.

MRS. MALAPROP: I am delighted with the scheme; never was anything better perpetrated![15]

CAPTAIN ABSOLUTE: But, pray, could not I see the lady for a few minutes now? I should like to try her temper a little.

MRS. MALAPROP: *(uncertainly)* Why, I don't know — I doubt she is not prepared for a visit of this kind. There is a decorum in these matters.

CAPTAIN ABSOLUTE: *(with confidence)* O Lord! she won't mind me — only tell her Beverley —

MRS. MALAPROP: *(sharply)* Sir!

CAPTAIN ABSOLUTE: *(aside)* Gently, good tongue.

MRS. MALAPROP: *(insistently)* What did you say of Beverley?

CAPTAIN ABSOLUTE: *(blandly)* Oh, I was going to pro-

---

[15] *Prepared.*

poses that you should tell her, by way of jest, that it was Beverley who was below; she'd come down fast enough then — ha! ha! ha!

MRS. MALAPROP: *(nodding)* 'Twould be a trick she well deserves; besides, you know the fellow tells her he'll get my consent to see her — ha! ha! Let him if he can, I say again. *(calling upstairs)* Lydia, come down here! *(to Captain Absolute)* He'll make me a go-between in their interviews! — ha! ha! ha! *(calling again while Captain Absolute is containing his explosive mirth with great difficulty)* Come down, I say, Lydia! *(perceiving Captain Absolute's merriment)* I don't wonder at your laughing, ha! ha! ha! — his impudence is truly ridiculous.

CAPTAIN ABSOLUTE: *(letting go a little)* 'Tis very ridiculous, upon my soul, ma'am, ha! ha! ha!

MRS. MALAPROP: *(annoyed)* The little hussy won't hear. Well, I'll go and tell her at once who it is — she shall know that Captain Absolute is come to wait on her. And I'll make her behave as becomes a young woman.

CAPTAIN ABSOLUTE: *(meekly)* As you please, ma'am.

MRS. MALAPROP: *(inclining her head as she leaves)* For the present, Captain, your servant. Ah! you're not done laughing yet, I see — elude my vigilance; yes, yes; ha! ha! ha! *(She goes out to right laughing sardonically.)*

CAPTAIN ABSOLUTE: *(releasing all restraint)* Ha! ha! ha! *(meditatively)* One would think now that I might throw off all disguise at once, and seize my prize with security; but such is Lydia's caprice, that to undeceive were probably to lose her. I'll see whether she knows me. *(turns to the back of the stage and seems intent on looking at the pictures.)*

LYDIA: *(entering from the right and talking to herseslf in smouldering exasperation)* What a scene am I now to go through! surely nothing can be more dreadful than to be obliged to listen to the loathsome addresses of a stranger to one's heart. I have heard of girls persecuted as I am, who have appealed in behalf of their favored lover to the generosity of his rival: suppose I were to try it — there stands the hated rival — an officer too! but oh, how unlike my Beverley! I wonder he don't begin — truly he seems a very negligent wooer! — quite at his ease, upon my word! — I'll speak first — Mr. Absolute.

CAPTAIN ABSOLUTE: *(turning around)* Ma'am.

LYDIA: O Heavens! Beverley!

CAPTAIN ABSOLUTE: Hush — hush, my life! softly! be not surprised!

LYDIA: *(nearly hysterical)* I am so astonished! and so terrified! and so overjoyed! — for Heaven's sake! how came you here?

CAPTAIN ABSOLUTE: *(as if understating his daring)* Briefly, I have deceived your aunt — I was informed that my new rival was to visit here this evening, and contriving to have him kept away, have passed myself on her for Captain Absolute.

LYDIA: *(delighted)* Oh, charming! and she really takes you for young Absolute!

CAPTAIN ABSOLUTE: Oh, she's convinced of it.

LYDIA: *(gaily)* ha! ha! ha! I can't forbear laughing to think how her sagacity is over-reached!

CAPTAIN ABSOLUTE: *(urgently)* But we trifle with our precious moments — such another opportunity may not occur; then let me now conjure my kind, my condescending angel, to fix the time when I may rescue her from undeserving persecution, and with a licensed warmth plead for my reward.

LYDIA: *(sentimentally)* Will you then, Beverley, consent to forfeit that portion of my paltry wealth? — that burden on the wings of love?

CAPTAIN ABSOLUTE: *(passionately)* Oh, come to me — rich only thus — in loveliness! Bring no portion to me but thy love — 'twill be generous in you, Lydia — for well you know, it is the only dower your poor Beverley can repay.

LYDIA: *(aside)* How persuasive are his words! — how charming will poverty be with him!

CAPTAIN ABSOLUTE: *(continuing with tender warmth)* Ah! my soul, what a life will we then live! Love shall be our idol and support! we will worship him with a monastic strictness; abjuring all worldly toys, to center every thought and action there. Proud of calamity, we will enjoy the wreck of wealth; while the surrounding gloom of adversity shall make the flame of our pure love show doubly bright. By Heavens! I would fling all goods of fortune from me with a prodigal hand, to enjoy the scene where I might clasp my Lydia to my bosom, and say, the world affords no smile to me but here. *(kisses her and holds her close. His back is at a slight angle between the door through which Lydia entered and the back of the stage. While embracing her, he looks over her shoulder and confesses to the audience.)* If she holds out now, the devil is in it!

LYDIA: *(turning her head momentarily to the audience — ecstatically)* How could I fly with him to the antipodes! *(As she turns back she perceives her aunt approaching the door as if about to enter. She stiffens and withdraws from Captain Absolute's embrace, speaking to herself with a frown)* But my persecution is not yet come to a crisis.

MRS. MALAPROP: *(stepping just inside the door, unperceived by Captain Absolute and ignored by Lydia, thinking aloud)* I am impatient to know how the little hussy deports herself.

CAPTAIN ABSOLUTE: *(not understanding her sudden withdrawal or the little frown on her face)* So pensive, Lydia! — is then your warmth abated?

MRS. MALAPROP: *(aside)* Warmth abated! — so! — she has been in a passion, I suppose.

LYDIA: *(dramatically)* No — nor ever can while I have life.

MRS. MALAPROP: *(aside)* An ill-tempered little devil! She'll be in a passion all her life — will she?

LYDIA: *(deliberately for her aunt's benefit)* Think not the idle threats of my ridiculous aunt can ever have any weight with me.

MRS. MALAPROP: *(aside)* Very dutiful, upon my word!

LYDIA: *(sighing deeply during Mrs. Malaprop's aside and continuing)* Let *her* choice be Captain Absolute, but

Beverley is mine. *(staring at Captain Absolute in pretended disdain)*

MRS. MALAPROP: *(aside)* I am astonished at her assurance! — to his face — this to his *face!*

CAPTAIN ABSOLUTE: *(kneeling before her)* Thus then let me enforce my suit.

MRS. MALAPROP: *(aside)* Aye, poor young man! — down on his knees entreating for pity! — I can contain no longer. *(sweeping into the center of the room)* Why, thou vixen! — I have overheard you.

CAPTAIN ABSOLUTE: *(aside)* Oh, confound her vigilance!

MRS. MALAPROP: Captain Absolute, I know not how to apologize for her shocking rudeness.

CAPTAIN ABSOLUTE: *(aside)* So all's safe, I find. *(to Mrs. Malaprop)* I have hopes, madam, that time will bring the young lady —

MRS. MALAPROP: *(interrupting angrily)* Oh, there's nothing to be hoped for from her! she's as headstrong as an allegory[16] on the banks of Nile.

LYDIA: *(argumentatively)* Nay, madam, what do you charge me with now?

MRS. MALAPROP: *(exasperated)* Why, thou unblushiing rebel — didn't you tell this gentleman to his face that you loved another better? — didn't you say you never would be his?

LYDIA: *(enjoying the situation so thoroughly that she is willing to risk discovery)* No, madam — I did not.

MRS. MALAPROP: *(impatiently)* Good Heavens! what assurance! — Lydia, Lydia, you ought to know that lying don't become a young woman — Didn't you boast that Beverley, that stroller Beverley, possessed your heart? Tell me that, I say.

LYDIA: *(histrionically)* 'Tis true, ma'am, and none but Beverley —

---

16 Probably her most famous malapropism; even what she meant makes little sense.

MRS. MALAPROP: *(sharply)* Hold! — hold! — Assurance! — you shall not be so rude.

CAPTAIN ABSOLUTE: *(placatingly)* Nay, pray, Mrs. Malaprop, don't stop the young lady's speech; she's very welcome to talk thus — it does not hurt me in the least, I assure you.

MRS. MALAPROP: You are too good captain — too amiably patient — but come with me, miss. Let me see you again soon, captain — remember what we have fixed.

CAPTAIN ABSOLUTE: *(cheerfully)* I shall, ma'am.

MRS. MALAPROP: *(to Lydia)* Come, take a graceful leave of the gentleman.

LYDIA: *(dewy-eyed)* May every blessing wait on my Beverley, my loved Bev——

MRS. MALAPROP: *(clapping her hand over Lydia's mouth and pushing her toward the right)* Hussy! I'll choke the word in your throat! — come along — come along. *(She shoves Lydia through the inner door to the right, giving her time only to glance back once to see Captain Absolute kissing his hand to her as he backs out of the outer door to the left.)*

Scene Four

The parlor of Bob Acres' lodgings in Bath. Acres has just been trying on newly acquired citified finery with the help of his servant David. His pink dress coat trimmed with silver, his pink silk breeches, white waistcoat, and while silk stockings are striking indeed. He struts back and forth, enormously pleased with his dandified appearance (actually half country race-track jockey and half town sharper), as the scene begins. David, a thorough country bumpkin in a dark brown square-cut livery coat and leather breeches, gapes at him in unqualified admiration.

ACRES: Indeed, David — do you think I become it so?

DAVID: *(enthusiastically)* You are quite another crea-

ture, believe me, master, by the mass! an we've any luck
we shall see the Devon monkerony[1] in all the printshops
in Bath!

ACRES: *(sententiously)* Dress does make a difference
David.

DAVID: *(simply)* 'Tis all in all, I think. — Difference!
why, an you were to go now to Clod Hall, I am certain
the old lady wouldn't know you: master Butler wouldn't
believe his own eyes, and Mrs. Pickle would cry, "Lard
presarve me!" Our dairy-maid would come giggling to
the door, and I warrant Dolly Tester, your honor's favorite, would blush like my waistcoat. — Oons! I'll hold
a gallon, there an't a dog in the house but would bark,
and I question whether Phillis would wag a hair of her
tail!

ACRES: *(gratified)* Aye, David, there's nothing like
polishing.

DAVID: *(ruefully)* So I says of your honor's boots; but
the boy never heeds me!

ACRES: *(practicing the new dance steps which he has
also just acquired)* But, David, has Mr. De-la-Grace been
here? I must rub up my balancing, and chasing, and
boring.

DAVID: I'll call again, sir.

ACRES: Do — and see if there are any letters for me
at the post-office.

DAVID: I will. *(lost in admiration at his master's new
wig)* By the mass, I can't help looking at your head! —
if I hadn't been by at the cooking, I wish I may die if I
should have known the dish again myself! *(He goes out
to the right, shaking his head.)*

ACRES: *(clumsily and awkwardly continuing to practice the new dance steps)* Sink, slide — coupee. — Confound the first inventors of cotillons! say I — they are as
bad as algebra to us country gentlemen. I can walk a
minuet easy enough when I am forced! — and I have
been accounted a good stick in a country-dance. Odds
jugs and tabors! I never valued your cross-over to couple

---

[1] A corruption of *macaroni,* a foppish man-about-town.

— figure in — right and left — and I'd foot it with e'er
a captain in the county! — but these outlandish heathen
allemandes and cotillons are quite beyond me! I shall
never prosper at 'em, that's sure — mine are true-born
English legs — they don't understand their curst French
lingo! — their *pas* this, and *pas* that, and *pas* t'other! —
damn me! my feet don't like to be called paws! No, 'tis
certain I have most Antigallican toes.

A servant enters at the right to announce a visitor.

SERVANT: Here is Sir Lucius O'Trigger to wait on you,
sir.

ACRES: *(pleased)* Show him in.

SIR LUCIUS: *(entering and speaking with sincere cordiality)* Mr. Acres, I am delighted to embrace you.

ACRES: *(conscious of his recently-acquired refinement)*
My dear Sir Lucius, I kiss your hands.

SIR LUCIUS: Pray, my friend, what has brought you
so suddenly to Bath?

ACRES: *(ruefully)* Faith! I have followed Cupid's Jack-
a-lantern, and find myself in a quagmire at last. In short,
I have been ill-used, Sir Lucius. I don't choose to mention names, but look on me as on a very ill-used gentleman.

SIR LUCIUS: *(with friendly concern)* Pray what is the
case? *(with delicacy)* I ask no names.

ACRES: *(in an aggrieved tone)* Mark me, Sir Lucius, I
fall as deep as need be in love with a young lady —
her friends take my part — I follow her to Bath — send
word of my arrival; and receive answer that the lady is
to be otherwise disposed of. — This, Sir Lucius, I call
being ill-used.

SIR LUCIUS: *(in wonderment)* Very ill, upon my conscience. — Pray, can you divine the cause of it?

ACRES: *(petulantly)* Why, there's the matter; she has
another lover, one Beverley, who, I am told, is now in
Bath. Odds slanders and lies! he must be at the bottom
of it.

SIR LUCIUS: *(musingly)* A rival in the case, is there?
— and you think he has supplanted you unfairly?

ACRES: *(with bravado)* Unfairly! to be sure he has. He never could have done it fairly.

SIR LUCIUS: *(energetically)* Then sure you know what is to be done!

ACRES: *(without an inkling)* Not I, upon my soul!

SIR LUCIUS: *(hinting broadly)* We wear no swords here,[2] but you understand me.

ACRES: *(faintly)* What! fight him!

SIR LUCIUS: *(vigorously)* Aye, to be sure; what can I mean else?

ACRES: *(hesitantly)* But he has given me no provocation.

SIR LUCIUS: Now I think he has given you the greatest provocation in the world. *(impassioned)* Can a man commit a more heinous offence against another than to fall in love with the same woman? Oh, by my soul! it is the most unpardonable breach of friendship.

ACRES: *(faintly catching the contagion of Sir Lucius's spirit)* Breach of friendship! aye, aye *(quickly cooling)* But I have no acquaintance with this man. I never saw him in my life.

SIR LUCIUS: *(pursuing his inverted logic)* That's no argument at all — he has the less right then to take such a liberty.

ACRES: *(fired again)* Gad, that's true — I grow full of anger, Sir Lucius! — I fire apace! Odds hilts and blades! I find a man may have a deal of valor in him and not know it! *(retreating)* But couldn't I contrive to have a little right on my side?

SIR LUCIUS: *(violently)* What the devil signifies right, when your honor is concerned? Do you think Achilles, or my little Alexander the Great, ever inquired where the right lay? No, by my soul, they drew their broadswords, and left the lazy sons of peace to settle the justice of it.

ACRES: *(in a gradual crescendo of counterfeit bravery)* Your words are a grenadier's march to my heart! I believe courage must be catching — I certainly do feel a kind of valor rising as it were — a kind of courage, as I

[2] An allusion to Beau Nash's rigorous prohibition.

may say. *(throwing off the last vestige of timidity)* Odds flints, pans, and triggers! I'll challenge him directly.

SIR LUCIUS: *(nostalgically)* Ah, my little friend, if I had Blunderbuss Hall here, I could show you a range of ancestry, in the O'Trigger line, that would furnish the new room; every one of whom had killed his man! For though the mansion-house and dirty acres have slipped through my fingers, I thank Heaven our honor and the family-pictures are as fresh as ever.

ACRES: *(in a glow of nobility)* O, Sir Lucius! I have had ancestors too! — every man of 'em colonel or captain in the militia! Odds balls and barrels! say no more — I'm braced for it. The thunder of your words has soured the milk of human kindness in my breast: — Zounds, as the man in the play says, *(topping an allusion to Lady Macbeth's description of her husband as "too full o' the milk of human kindness" and to her own milk as "gall" with a misquotation of Hamlet's "Now could I drink hot blood, and do such bitter business as the day would quake to look on.")* I could do such deeds!

SIR LUCIUS: *(restraining him)* Come, come, there must be no passion at all in the case — these things should always be done civilly.

ACRES: *(defensively)* I *must* be in a passion, Sir Lucius — I *must* be in a rage. *(entreatingly)* Dear Sir Lucius let me be in a rage, if you love me. *(rushing to the desk and seizing pen and paper to write the challenge while still in the mood)* Come, here's pen and paper. I would the ink were red! *(sits down and holds the pen poised impatiently over the paper)* Indite. I say indite! — How shall I begin? Odds bullets and blades! I'll write a good bold hand, however.

SIR LUCIUS: *(attempting to restrain this sudden frenzy)* Pray compose yourself.

ACRES: *(impatiently)* Come — now, shall I begin with an oath? Do, Sir Lucius, let me begin with a *damme*.

SIR LUCIUS: Pho! pho! do the thing decently, and like a Christain. Begin now — *Sir* —

ACRES: That's too civil by half.

SIR LUCIUS: *(dictating as Acres writes) To prevent the confusion that might arise —*

ACRES: *(scribbling rapidly)* Well —

SIR LUCIUS: *From our both addressing the same lady —*

ACRES: *(enthusiastically)* Aye, there's the reason — *(writing) same lady —* Well —

SIR LUCIUS: *I shall expect the honor of your company —*

ACRES: *(stopping his writing abruptly and looking up in abysmal ignorance of the etiquette of duelling)* Zounds! I'm not asking him to dinner.

SIR LUCIUS: *(in a mollifying tone)* Pray be easy.

ACRES: Well, then, *(writing) — honor of your company —*

SIR LUCIUS: *To settle our pretensions —*

ACRES: Well.

SIR LUCIUS: *(meditatively)* Let me see, aye, King's-Mead-Fields will do — *(dictating) in King's-Mead-Fields.*

ACRES: *(scrawling the last words with a flourish)* So, that's done. Well, I'll fold it up presently; with my own crest — a hand and dagger — shall be the seal.

SIR LUCIUS: You see now this little explanation will put a stop at once to all confusion or misunderstanding that might arise between you.

ACRES: *(contentedly and with no suspicion of the absurdity involved)* Aye, we fight to prevent any misunderstanding.

SIR LUCIUS: *(practically)* Now, I'll leave you to fix your own time. Take my advice, and you'll decide it this evening if you can; then let the worst come of it, 'twill be off your mind to-morrow.

ACRES: *(nodding agreement)* Very true.

SIR LUCIUS: *(continuing)* So I shall see nothing more of you, unless it be by letter, till the evening. I would do myself the honor to carry your message; but, to tell you a secret, I believe I shall have just such another affair on my own hands. There is a gay captain here, who put a jest on me lately, at the expense of my country, and I only want to fall in with the gentleman to call him out.

ACRES: *(eagerly)* By my valor, I should like to see you fight first! Odds life! I should like to see you kill him, if it was only to get a little lesson.

SIR LUCIUS: *(grandly)* I shall be very proud of instructing you. *(starting to leave)* Well, for the present — but remember now, when you meet your antagonist, do everything in a mild and agreeable manner. Let your courage be as keen, but as the same time as polished as your sword. *(He leaves at the right and Acres retires to his bedroom to the left.)*

ACT FOUR

Scene One

The same, shortly thereafter. David has returned from his errand and has just shared the confidence of his master concerning the impending duel. Acres and David are discussing the affair as the scene beings.

DAVID: *(in fearful admiration)* Then, by the mass, sir! *I* would do no such thing — ne'er a Sir Lucius O'-Trigger in the kingdom should make me fight, when I wa'n't so minded. *(remembering Acres' mother)* Oons! what will the old lady say, when she hears o't?

ACRES: *(with reckless bravado)* Ah! David, if you had heard Sir Lucius! Odds sparks and flames! he would have roused your valor.

DAVID: *(demurring)* Not he, indeed. I hate such blood-thirsty cormorants. Look'ee, master, if you'd wanted a bout at boxing, quarter-staff, or short-staff, I should never be the man to bid you cry off: but for your curst sharps and snaps,[1] I never knew any good to come of 'em.

ACRES: *(protesting vigorously)* But my honor, David, my honor! I must be very careful of my honor.

DAVID: *(practically)* Aye, by the mass! and I would be *very* careful of it; and I think in return my honor couldn't do less than to be very careful of me.

ACRES: *(with noble indignation)* Odds blades! David, no gentleman will ever risk the loss of his honor.

DAVID: *(persistently and echoing the soliloquy of Shakespeare's Falstaff of* Henry IV*)* I say then, it would be but civil in honor never to risk the loss of a gentleman.

---

[1] Swords or rapiers and pistols.

Look'ee, master, this honor seems to me to be a marvellous false friend: aye, truly, a very courtier-like servant. — Put the case, I was a gentleman *(which, thank God, no one can say of me);* well — my honor makes me quarrel with another gentleman of my acquaintance. — So — we fight. (Pleasant enough that!) Boh! I kill him — (the more's my luck!) now, pray who gets the profit of it? — Why, my honor. But put the case that he kills me! — by the mass! I go to the worms, and my honor whips over to my enemy.

ACRES: *(correcting him)* No, David — in that case — Odds crowns and laurels! — your honor follows you to the grave.

DAVID: *(emphatically)* Now that's *just* the place where I could make a shift to do without it.

ACRES: *(inwardly wincing under David's suggestions)* Zounds! David, you are a coward! — It doesn't become my valor to listen to you. What, shall I disgrace my ancestors? Think of that, David — think what it would be to disgrace my ancestors!

DAVID: *(with humble reasonableness)* Under favor, the surest way of not disgracing them is to keep as long as you can out of their company. Look'ee now, master, to go to them in such haste — with an ounce of lead in your brains — I should think might as well be let alone. Our ancestors are very good kind of folks; but they are the last people I should choose to have a visiting acquaintance with.

ACRES: *(weakening)* But, David, now, you don't think there is such very, very, *very* great danger, hey? *(cheerfully)* Odds life! people often fight without any mischief done!

DAVID: *(lugubriously)* By the mass, I think 'tis ten to one against you! — Oons! here to meet some lion-headed fellow, I warrant, with his damned double-barrelled swords, and cut-and-thrust pistols! — Lord bless us! it makes me tremble to think o't. Those be such desperate bloody-minded weapons! Well, I never could abide 'em — from a child I never could fancy 'em! — I suppose there an't been so merciless a beast in the world as your loaded pistol!

ACRES: *(badly shaken, his voice squeaking with the strain of affected bravery)* Zounds! I *won't* be afraid! — Odds fire and fury! you shan't make me afraid. *(holding the challenge out to him)* Here is the challenge, and I have sent for my dear friend Jack Absolute to carry it for me.

DAVID: *(shrinking back)* Aye, i' the name of mischief, let him be the messenger. — For my part, I wouldn't lend a hand to it for the best horse in your stable. *(eyeing the note gingerly)* By the mass! it don't look like another letter. It is, as I may say, a designing and malicious-looking letter; and I warrant smells of gunpowder like a soldier's pouch! — *(sniffing it and jumping back)* Oons! I wouldn't swear it mayn't go off.

ACRES:*(laughing nervously)* Out, you poltroon! you ha'n't the valor of a grasshopper.

DAVID: *(somberly)* Well, I say no more — 'twill be sad news, to be sure, at Clod Hall! but I ha' done. *(funerally)* How Phillis will howl when she hears of it! — Aye, poor bitch, she little thinks what shooting her master's going after! And I warrant old Crop, who has carried your honor, field and road, these ten years, will curse the hour he was born. *(whimpering)*

ACRES:*(uncertainly)* It won't do, David — I am *determined* to fight — so get along, you coward, *(shakily)* while I'm in the mind.

A servant enters from the right to announce a visitor.

SERVANT: Captain Absolute, sir.

ACRES: *(relieved at the thought of company)* Oh! show him up. *(The servant leaves.)*

DAVID: *(mournfully)* Well, Heaven send we be all alive this time to-morrow.

ACRES: *(still jittery but gaining courage at the thought of Captain Absolute's backing)* What's that? — Don't provoke me, David!

DAVID: *(whimpering and calling from the door as he leaves to the left)* Good-bye, master.

ACRES: *(shouting after him)* Get along, you cowardly, dastardly, croaking raven!

CAPTAIN ABSOLUTE: *(entering from the right)* What's the matter, Bob?

ACRES: *(as if only half-aware of his guest and still looking after David)* A vile, sheep-hearted blockhead! If I hadn't the valor of St. George and the dragon to boot —

CAPTAIN ABSOLUTE: *(insistently)* But what did you want with me, Bob?

ACRES: *(turning suddenly as if surprised)* Oh! *(dramatically thrusting the challenge toward Captain Absolute)* There!

CAPTAIN ABSOLUTE: *(taking it and reading the inscription)* To Ensign Beverley. *(aside)* So — what's going on now! *(to Acres)* Well, what's this?

ACRES: *(solemnly)* A challenge!

CAPTAIN ABSOLUTE: *(wonderingly)* Indeed! Why, you won't *fight* him; will you, Bob.

ACRES: *(heroically)* Egad, but I will Jack. Sir Lucius has wrought me to it. He has left me full of rage — and I'll fight this evening, that so much good passion mayn't be wasted.

CAPTAIN ABSOLUTE: *(suspecting Acres of knowing the identity of Ensign Beverley)* But what have *I* to do with this?

ACRES: Why, as I think you know something of this fellow, I want you to find him out for me, and give him this mortal defiance.

CAPTAIN ABSOLUTE: *(relieved)* Well, give it to me, and trust me he gets it.

ACRES: *(with overdone gratitude)* Thank you, my dear friend, my dear Jack; but it is giving you a great deal of trouble.

CAPTAIN ABSOLUTE: *(drily)* Not in the least — I beg you won't mention it. — No trouble in the world, I assure you.

ACRES: *(ecstatically)* You are very kind. — What it is to have a friend! *(tentatively)* You couldn't be my second, could you, Jack?

CAPTAIN ABSOLUTE: *(thoughtfully)* Why no, Bob —
not in *this* affair — it would not be quite so proper.

ACRES: *(disappointed)* Well, then, I must get my friend
Sir Lucius. *(imploringly)* I shall have your good wishes,
however, Jack?

CAPTAIN ABSOLUTE: *(with hearty earnestness)* Whenever he meets you, believe me.

The servant enters again with a message.

SERVANT: Sir Anthony Absolute is below, inquiring for
the captain.

CAPTAIN ABSOLUTE:*(to the servant)* I'll come instantly.
(The servant bows and disappears) Well, my little hero
— *(holding out his hand to Acres in leave-taking)* success attend you. *(makes as if to go)*

ACRES: *(nervously)* Stay — Stay, Jack — If Beverley
should ask you what kind of a man your friend Acres is,
do tell him I am a devil of a fellow — *(entreatingly)* will
you Jack?

CAPTAIN ABSOLUTE: *(heartily)* To be sure I shall. I'll
say you are a determined dog — hey, Bob?

ACRES: *(eagerly)* Aye, do, do — and if that frightens
him, egad, perhaps he mayn't come. So tell him I generally kill a man a week; will you, Jack.

CAPTAIN ABSOLUTE: I will, I will; I'll say you are called
in the country "Fighting Bob."

ACRES: *(sensing dimly that his courage is ebbing
away)* Right — right — 'tis all to prevent mischief; for
I don't want to take his life if I clear my honor.

CAPTAIN ABSOLUTE: *(sardonically)* No! — that's very
kind of you.

ACRES: *(taken aback)* Why, you don't wish me to kill
him — do you Jack?

CAPTAIN ABSOLUTE: *(with heavy emphasis on every
word)* No, upon my soul, I do not. *(lightly as he moves
left toward the door)* But a devil of a fellow, hey?

ACRES: *(unwilling to relinquish his friend's moral support)* True, true — but stay — stay, Jack, — you may
add, that you never saw me in such a rage before — a
most devouring rage!

CAPTAIN ABSOLUTE: *(amused but anxious to leave)* I will, I will.

ACRES: *(anxiously with a forlorn expression)* Remember, Jack — a determined dog.

CAPTAIN ABSOLUTE: *(shouting back cheerfully as he goes out to right)* Aye, aye, "Fighting Bob!" *(Acres looks after him with a somewhat quizzical expression, shakes his head faintly with a trace of bewilderment, and goes out to the left.)*

Scene Two

The parlor of Mrs. Malaprop's lodgings. Mrs. Malaprop and Lydia are conversing as an aftermath of Captain Absolute's recent visit. The conversation is somewhat heated; both are standing.

MRS. MALAPROP: *(with irritation)* Why, thou perverse one! — tell me what you can object to him? Isn't he a handsome man? — tell me that. A genteel man? a pretty figure of a man?

LYDIA: *(aside)* She little thinks whom she is praising! *(pertly to her aunt)* So is Beverley, ma'am.

MRS. MALAPROP: *(severely)* No caparisons,[1] miss, if you please. Caparisons don't become a young woman. No! Captain Absolute is indeed a fine gentleman!

LYDIA: *(aside)* Aye, the Captain Absolute you have seen.

MRS. MALAPROP: *(carried away by her admiration of the Captain)* Then he's so well bred; — so full of alacrity, and adulation![2] — and has so much to say for himself: — in such good language too! His physiognomy[3] so grammatical! Then his presence is so noble! I protest, when I saw him, I thought of what Hamlet says in the play: —

---

[1] Comparisons.

[2] Her intended meaning here is anybody's guess.

[3] Phraseology.

"Hesperian curls — the front of Job himself! —
An eye, like March to threaten at command! —
A station, like Harry Mercury, new —"

(groping for the next line) — Something about kissing —
on a hill —[4] — however, the similitude[5] struck me
directly.

LYDIA:*(aside)* How enraged she'll be presently, when
she discovers her mistake!

A servant enters from the left to announce visitors.

SERVANT: Sir Anthony and Captain Absolute are below, ma'am.

MRS. MALAPROP: Show them up here. *(The servant
leaves as Mrs. Malaprop turns to Lydia)* Now, Lydia, I
insist on your behaving as becomes a young woman.
Show your good breeding, at least, though you have forgot your duty.

LYDIA: *(with cold disdain)* Madam, I have told you my
resolution! — I shall not only give him no encourage-
ment, but I won't even speak to, or look at him. *(She
stalks with determination to the right-hand corner of the
room, turns a chair around, and plants herself in it,
rigidly facing the wall.)*

*Sir Anthony enters, ushering in his son, before Mrs.
Malaprop has a chance to object to Lydia's uncivil behavior.*

SIR ANTHONY: *(in the grand manner)* Here we are, Mrs.
Malaprop; come to mitigate the frowns of unrelenting
beauty, — and difficulty enough I had to bring this fellow. I don't know what's the matter; but if I had not held
him by force, he'd have given me the slip.

MRS. MALAPROP: *(graciously)* You have infinite trouble, Sir Anthony, in the affair. *(with embarrassment)* I am

---

[4] Mrs. Malaprop's rendition of these lines can be fully appre-
ciated only by comparing them with the original:

"Hyperion's curls, the front of Jove himself,
An eye, like Mars, to threaten or command,
A station like the herald Mercury
New-lighted on a heaven-kissing hill."

[5] *Simile* or *similarity* depending on what she is referring to.

ashamed for the cause! *(in an anguished stage-whisper to Lydia)* Lydia, Lydia, rise, I beseech you! — pay your respects!

SIR ANTHONY: *(addressing Mrs. Malaprop but speaking loudly for the obvious benefit of Lydia)* I hope, madam, that Miss Languish has reflected on the worth of this gentleman, and the regard due to her aunt's choice, and my alliance. *(whispering urgently to his son)* Now, Jack, speak to her!

CAPTAIN ABSOLUTE: *(aside)* What the devil shall I do! *(quietly to his father)* You, see, sir, she won't even look at me, whilst you are here. I knew she wouldn't! I told you so. Let me entreat you, sir, to leave us together!

LYDIA: *(aside as Captain Absolute whispers to his father)* I wonder I ha'n't heard my aunt exclaim yet! sure she can't have looked at him! — perhaps their regimentals are alike, and she is something blind.

SIR ANTHONY: *(to his son)* I say, sir, I won't stir a foot yet!

MRS. MALAPROP: I am sorry to say, Sir Anthony, that my affluence[6] over my niece is very small. *(aside to Lydia)* Turn around, Lydia: I blush for you!

SIR ANTHONY: *(looking toward Lydia)* May I not flatter myself that Miss Languish will assign what cause of dislike she can have to my son! *(aside to Captain Absolute)* Why don't you begin, Jack? — Speak, you puppy — speak!

MRS. MALAPROP: It is impossible, Sir Anthony, she can have any. She will not say she has. *(aside to Lydia, hissing)* Answer, hussy! why don't you answer?

SIR ANTHONY: *(maintaining a pretence of composure)* Then, madam, I trust that a childish and hasty predilection will be no bar to Jack's happiness. *(aside to Captain Absolute, angrily)* Zounds! sirrah! why don't you speak?

LYDIA: *(aside, wondering)* I think my lover seems as little inclined to conversation as myself. — How strangely blind my aunt must be!

CAPTAIN ABSOLUTE: *(sufficiently impressed by the*

---

[6] Influence.

awkwardness of the occasion and his father's suppressed wrath to attempt to appear dutiful, but speaking in an unnatural tone of voice) Hem! hem! madam — hem! *(His attempt chokes in his throat, and he turns nervously to his father.)* Faith! sir, I am so confounded! — and — so — so — confused! — I told you I should be so, sir — I knew it. The — the — tremor of my passion entirely takes away my presence of mind.

SIR ANTHONY: *(peremptorily)* But it don't take away your voice, fool, does it? — Go up, and speak to her directly!

Captain Absolute makes signs to Mrs. Malaprop to leave them alone together.

MRS. MALAPROP: *(archly responding to the cue)* Sir Anthony, shall we leave them together? *(aside to Lydia in utter exasperation)* Ah! you stubborn little vixen!

SIR ANTHONY: Not yet, ma'am, not yet! *(aside to Captain Absolute)* What the devil are you at? Unlock your jaws, sirrah, or —

CAPTAIN ABSOLUTE: *(aside)* Now Heaven send she may be too sullen to look round! — I must disguise my voice. *(draws near Lydia, and speaks in a low hoarse tone)* Will not Miss Languish lend an ear to the mild accents of true love? Will not —

SIR ANTHONY: *(interrupting violently)* What the devil ails the fellow? Why don't you speak out? — not stand croaking like a frog in a quinsy!

CAPTAIN ABSOLUTE: *(even more frog-like than before)* The — the — excess of my awe, and my — my — my modesty, quite choke me!

SIR ANTHONY: *(completely nonplussed)* Ah, your modesty again! *(tensely)* I'll tell you what, Jack; if you don't speak out directly, and glibly too, I shall be in such a rage! *(rather bitingly to Mrs. Malaprop)* Mrs. Malaprop, I wish the lady would favor us with something more than a side-front. *(Mrs. Malaprop gestures frantically to Lydia to turn around.)*

CAPTAIN ABSOLUTE: *(aside)* So all will out, I see! *(Lydia makes no response to Mrs. Malaprop's gesturing. Cap-*

*tain Absolute moves quietly up to the back of her chair
and speaks to her very softly and urgently.)* Be not surprised, my Lydia, suppress all surprise at present.

LYDIA: *(aside, amazed)* Heavens! 'tis Beverley's voice!
Sure he can't have imposed on Sir Anthony too! *(gradually turns her head until she sees Captain Absolute, then
leaps to her feet with astonished delight)* Is this possible!
— my Beverley! — how can this be? — my Beverley?

CAPTAIN ABSOLUTE: *(aside in total resignation)* Ah!
'tis all over.

SIR ANTHONY: *(outraged)* Beverley! — the devil —
Beverley! — What can the girl mean? This is my son,
Jack Absolute.

MRS. MALAPROP: *(convinced that Lydia is deliberately
staging a scene)* For shame, hussy! for shame! your head
runs so on that fellow, that you have him always in your
eyes! — beg Captain Absolute's pardon directly.

LYDIA: *(starry-eyed)* I see no Captain Absolute, but my
loved Beverley!

SIR ANTHONY: *(completely baffled)* Zounds! the girl's
mad! — her brain's turned by reading.

MRS. MALAPROP: *(equally bewildered)* O' my conscience, I believe so! *(sharply to Lydia)* What do you
mean by Beverley, hussy? You saw Captain Absolute before today; there he is — your husband that shall be.

LYDIA: *(soulfully)* With all my soul, ma'am — when I
refuse my Beverley —

SIR ANTHONY: Oh! she's as mad as Bedlam! *(seized by
the ghost of an idea)* Or has this fellow been playing us
a rogue's trick! *(suspiciously to Captain Absolute)* Come
here, sirrah, who the devil are you?

CAPTAIN ABSOLUTE: *(with deliberate uncertainty)* Faith,
sir, I am not quite clear myself; *(obediently)* but I'll endeavor to recollect.

SIR ANTHONY: *(pretending paternal anger but secretly
amused by his suspicion of his son's duplicity)* Are you
my son or not? Answer for your mother, you dog, if you
won't for me.

MRS. MALAPROP: *(hazily beginning to see through the*

clouds) Aye, sir, who are you? O mercy! I begin to suspect —

CAPTAIN ABSOLUTE: *(aside)* Ye powers of impudence, befriend me! *(humbly to his father)* Sir Anthony, most assuredly I am your wife's son; and that I sincerely believe myself to be yours also, I hope my duty has always shown. *(graciously to Mrs. Malaprop)* Mrs. Malaprop, I am your most respectful admirer, and shall be proud to add affectionate nephew. I need not tell my Lydia that she sees her faithful Beverley, who, knowing the singular generosity of her temper, assumed that name and station which has proved a test of the most disinterested love, which he now hopes to enjoy in a more elevated character.

LYDIA: *(sullenly)* So! — there will be no elopement after all!

SIR ANTHONY: *(delighted)* Upon my soul, Jack, thou art a very impudent fellow! to do you justice, I think I never saw a piece of more consummate assurance!

CAPTAIN ABSOLUTE: *(acknowledging this parental praise in an assured manner)* Oh, you flatter me, sir — you compliment — 'tis my modesty, you know, sir, — my modesty that has stood in my way.

SIR ANTHONY: *(affectionately)* Well, I am glad you are not the dull, insensible varlet you pretended to be, however! I'm glad you have made a fool of your father, you dog — I am. *(with indulgent accusations)* So this was your *penitence,* your *duty* and *obedience!* — I thought it was sudden! — *You never heard their names before,* not *you! — What the Languishes of Worcestershire,* hey? — *if you could please me in the affair, it was all you desired!* — Ah! you dissembling villain! *(vastly enjoying the situation)* What! — *(pointing to Lydia) She squints,* don't she? — *a little red-haired girl!* — hey? — Why, you hypocritical young rascal! — I wonder you a'n't ashamed to hold up your head!

CAPTAIN ABSOLUTE: *(still rather cocky but with understandably mixed emotions)* 'Tis with difficulty, sir. I am confused — very much confused, as you must percieve.

MRS. MALAPROP: *(pained by the dawning revelation)*

O Lud! Sir Anthony! — a new light breaks in upon me!
— hey! — how! — what! Captain, did you write the letters then? — What — am I to thank *you* for the elegant
compilation⁷ of *an old weather-beaten she-dragon* — hey!
— O mercy! — was it you that reflected on my parts
of speech?

CAPTAIN ABSOLUTE: *(appealing to his father)* Dear, sir!
my modesty will be overpowered at last, if you don't as-
sist me. — I shall certainly not be able to stand it!

SIR ANTHONY:*(broadly)* Come, come, Mrs. Malaprop,
we must forget and forgive; — odds life! matters have
taken so clever a turn all of a sudden, that I could find in
my heart to be so good-humored! *(flirtatiously)* and so
gallant! hey! Mrs. Malaprop!

MRS. MALAPROP: *(completely thawed)* Well, Sir Anthony, since you desire it, we will not anticipate the past;
— so mind, young people — our retrospection⁸ will be
all to the future.

SIR ANTHONY: *(heartily)* Come, we must leave them together; Mrs. Malaprop, they long to fly into each other's
arms, I warrant! *(roguishly to his son)* Jack, isn't the
cheek as I said, hey; — and the eye, you rogue! — and
the lip — hey? *(with exalted good-humor)* Come, Mrs.
Malaprop, we'll not disturb their tenderness — theirs is
the time of life for happiness! — *(breaking into the opening of a song from Gay's "Beggar's Opera")* Youth's the
season made for joy — (ecstatically) Hey! — Odds life!
I'm in such spirits, — I don't know what I could not do!
(gallantly giving his hand to Mrs. Malaprop) Permit me,
ma'am. *(fatuously)* Tol-de rol — 'gad, I should like to
have a little fooling myself.—Tol-de-rol! de-rol. *(Execut-
ing clumsy but elated dance steps, he escorts Mrs. Malaprop flambuoyantly out of the room to the right. Lydia,
haughty and sullen, continues to sit fixed in her chair.)*

CAPTAIN ABSOLUTE: *(aside)* So much thought bodes me
no good. *(beseechingly, to Lydia)* So grave, Lydia?

---

⁷ Appellation.

⁸ Here she is only mildly confused in reversing the meanings of
anticipate and *retrospection*.

LYDIA:*(haughtily)* Sir!

CAPTAIN ABSOLUTE: *(aside)* So! — egad! I thought as much! — that monosyllable has froze me! *(reasonably to Lydia)* What, Lydia, now that we are as happy in our friends' consent, as in our mutual vows —

LYDIA: *(peevishly)* Friends' consent, indeed!

CAPTAIN ABSOLUTE: *(as if addressing a child)* Come, come, we must lay aside some of our romance — *(ironically)* — a little wealth and comfort may be endured after all. *(in a matter-of-fact tone)* And for your fortune, the lawyers shall make such settlements as —

LYDIA: *(interrupting passionately)* Lawyers! I hate lawyers!

CAPTAIN ABSOLUTE: *(agreeably)* Nay, then, we will not wait for their lingering forms, but instantly procure the licence, and —

LYDIA: *(cutting him off sharply)* The licence! — I hate licence!

CAPTAIN ABSOLUTE: *(in wheedling entreaty)* Oh my love! be not so unkind! *(dramatically kneeling beside her)* Thus let me entreat!

LYDIA: *(bitterly)* Phsaw! — what signifies kneeling, when you know I must have you?

CAPTAIN ABSOLUTE: *(rising with hurt pride and dignity)* Nay, madam, there shall be no constraint upon your inclinations, I promise you. If I have lost your heart, I resign the rest. *(aside)* 'Gad, I must try what a little spirit will do.

LYDIA: *(getting up from her chair and matching his carefully staged dignity with a genuinely dignified accusation of her own)* Then, sir, let me tell you, the interest you had there was acquired by a mean, unmanly imposition, and deserves the punishment of fraud. What, you have been treating me like a child! — humoring my romance! and laughing, I suppose, at your success!

CAPTAIN ABSOLUTE: *(earnestly)* You wrong me, Lydia, you wrong me — only hear —

LYDIA: *(deeply moved and indulging herself in a finely theatrical mood of betrayed innocence.)* So, while I fondly imagined we were deceiving my relations, and flattered myself that I should outwit and incense them all — behold! my hopes are to be crushed at once, by my aunt's consent and approbation — and I am myself the only dupe at last! *(walking up and down in front of her lover as she distractedly gropes for and then extracts a miniature portrait from her bosom)* But here, sir, here is the picture — *Beverley's* picture! which I have worn, night and day, in spite of threats and entreaties! *(flings it at him)* There, sir; and be assured I throw the original from my heart as easily.

CAPTAIN ABSOLUTE: *(accepting his fate)* Nay, nay, ma'am, we will not differ as to that. — Here, *(taking out a picture)* here is Miss Lydia Languish. *(He gazes at it rapturously.)* What a difference! *(with steadily increasingly ardor)* Aye, there is the heavenly assenting smile, that first gave soul and spirit to my hopes! — those are the lips which sealed a vow, as yet scarce dry in Cupid's calendar! and there the half-resentful blush, that would have checked the ardor of my thanks! *(sighing fatalistically)* Well, all that's past! — all over indeed! *(holds the picture as if to duplicate her action by flinging it from him)* There, madam — in beauty, that copy is not equal to you, *(as if checking the impulse as he studies the portrait more carefully)* but in my mind its merit over the original, in being still the same, *(with a catch in his voice)* is such — that — I cannot find in my heart to part with it. *(puts it back again)*

LYDIA: *(softening)* 'Tis your own doing, sir. *(speaking with difficulty)* I — I —I suppose you are perfectly satisfied.

CAPTAIN ABSOLUTE: *(with emphatic and heart-broken irony)* O, most certainly — sure, now, this is much better than being in love — ha! ha! ha! — there's some spirit in this! — What signifies breaking some scores of solemn promises: — all that's of no consequence, you know. — To be sure people will say, that Miss didn't know her own mind — but never mind that! Or perhaps, they may be ill-natured enough to hint that the gentleman grew tired of the lady and forsook her — but don't let that fret you.

LYDIA: There is no bearing his insolence. *(bursts into tears)*

Mrs. Malaprop and Sir Anthony reenter, both looking very smug and pleased with the world.

MRS. MALAPROP: *(coyly)* Come, we must interrupt your billing and cooing awhile.

LYDIA: *(sobbing)* This is worse than your treachery and deceit, you base ingrate!

SIR ANTHONY: What the devil's the matter now! — Zounds! Mrs. Malaprop, this is the oddest billing and cooing I have ever heard! — but what the deuce is the meaning of it? I am quite astonished.

CAPTAIN ABSOLUTE: *(with frozen dignity)* Ask the lady, sir.

MRS. MALAPROP: *(utterly bewildered by Lydia's tears after having been left alone with the man of her heart's desire)* Oh, mercy! — I'm quite analyzed[9] for my part! Why, Lydia, what is the reason for this?

LYDIA: *(imitating the frozen accents of Captain Absolute)* Ask the gentleman, ma'am.

SIR ANTHONY: Zounds! I shall be in a frenzy. *(slyly to Captain Absolute)* Why, Jack, you are not come out to be any one else, are you?

MRS. MALAPROP: *(half seriously)* Aye, sir, there's no more trick, is there? — you are not like Cerberus,[10] three gentlemen at once, are you?

CAPTAIN ABSOLUTE: *(protesting)* You'll not let me speak — *(self-righteously)* I say the lady can account for this much better than I can.

LYDIA: *(haughtily)* Ma'am, you once commanded me never to think of Beverley again — there is the man — I now obey you: for, from this moment, I renounce him for ever. *(She sweeps out of the room.)*

MRS. MALAPROP: *(at her wit's end)* O mercy! and miracles! what a turn here is — *(to Captain Absolute, sus-*

---

9 Paralyzed.

10 The three-headed watchdog of Hades.

piciously) Why sure, Captain, you haven't behaved disrespectfully to my niece.

SIR ANTHONY: *(with boisterous amusement)* Ha! ha! ha! — ha! ha! ha! now I see it. Ha! ha! ha! — now I see it — you have been too lively, Jack.

CAPTAIN ABSOLUTE: *(affronted)* Nay, sir, upon my word —

SIR ANTHONY: Come, no lying, Jack — I'm sure 'twas so.

MRS. MALAPROP: *(embarrassed)* O Lud! Sir Anthony! — O fie, Captain!

CAPTAIN ABSOLUTE: *(earnestly)* Upon my soul, ma'am—

SIR ANTHONY: *(with hearty approval)* Come, no excuses, Jack; why, your father, you rogue, was so before you! — the blood of the Absolutes was always impatient. — Ha! ha! ha! poor little Lydia! why you've frightened her, you dog, you have.

CAPTAIN ABSOLUTE: *(continuing to protest)* By all that's good, sir —

SIR ANTHONY: *(irately)* Zounds! say no more, I tell you. Mrs. Malaprop shall make your peace. *(casually to Mrs. Malaprop)* You must make his peace, Mrs. Malaprop: — you must tell her 'tis Jack's way — tell her 'tis all our ways — it runs in the blood of our family! *(turning to leave)* Come away, Jack. — Ha! ha! ha! *(bowing low to Mrs. Malaprop)* Mrs. Malaprop — a young villian! *(pushes Captain Absolute before him out of the door to left.)*

MRS. MALAPROP: *(blushing and going out to right after Lydia)* O! Sir Anthony! — O fie, Captain!

Scene Three

The North Parade. Sir Lucius O'Trigger strolls on from the left, peering about and obviously looking for someone.

SIR LUCIUS: *(talking to himself)* I wonder where this Captain Absolute hides himself! Upon my conscience!

these officers are always in one's way in love affairs. *(musingly)* I remember I might have married Lady Dorothy Carmine, if it had not been for a little rogue of a major who ran away with her before she could get a sight of me! *(huffily)* And I wonder too what it is the ladies can see in them to be so fond of them — unless it be a touch of the old serpent in 'em, that makes the little creatures be caught, like vipers, with a bit of red cloth. *(looking up sharply)* Hah! isn't this the Captain coming? — *(gazing across the stage into the right wings)* Faith, it is! *(with irritation)* There is a probability of succeeding about that fellow that is mighty provoking! Who the devil is he talking to? *(He moves to the back of the stage as Captain Absolute enters, giving voice to his anger over Lydia's recent behavior.)*

CAPTAIN ABSOLUTE: To what fine purpose I have been plotting! a noble reward for all my schemes, upon my soul; — a little gypsy! — I did not think her romance could have made her so absurd either. *(in an angry outburst)* 'Sdeath, I never was in a worse humor in my life! — I could cut my own throat, or any other person's, with the greatest pleasure in the world!

SIR LUCIUS: *(delighted with the Captain's mood)* Oh, faith! I'm in the luck of it. I could never have found him in a sweeter temper for my purpose — *(his brogue deepening in anticipation of a quarrel)* To be sure, I'm just come in the nick! Now to enter into conversation with him, and so quarrel genteelly. *(He strolls arrogantly forward and places himself directly in front of Captain Absolute.)* With regard to that matter, captain — *(in a loud and detemined voice)* I must beg leave to differ in opinion with you.

CAPTAIN ABSOLUTE: *(surprised and taken aback)* Upon my word, then, you must be a very subtle disputant: — because, sir, I happened just then to be having no opinion at all.

SIR LUCIUS: *(pugnaciously)* That's no reason. For give me leave to tell you, a man may think an untruth as well as speak one.

CAPTAIN ABSOLUTE: *(moderately but with firmness)* Very true, sir; but if a man never utters his thoughts, I should think they might stand a chance of escaping controversy.

SIR LUCIUS: *(with determined arrogance)* Then, sir, you differ in opinion with me, which amounts to the same thing.

CAPTAIN ABSOLUTE: *(angered)* Hark'ee, Sir Lucius; if I had not before known you to be a gentleman, upon my soul, I should not have discovered it at this interview: for what you can drive at, unless you mean to quarrel with me, I cannot conceive!

SIR LUCIUS: *(with heavy sarcasm)* I humbly thank you, sir, for the quickness of your apprehension. *(with a low bow)* You have named the very thing I would be at.

CAPTAIN ABSOLUTE: Very well, sir; I shall certainly not balk your inclinations. — But I should be glad you would please to explain your motives.

SIR LUCIUS: *(a purist in these matters)* Pray, sir, be easy — the quarrel is a very pretty quarrel as it stands — we should only spoil it by trying to explain it. However, your memory is very short, or you could not have forgot an affront you passed on me within this week. So, no more, but name your time and place.

CAPTAIN ABSOLUTE: *(stiffly but wearily)* Well, sir, since you are so bent on it, the sooner the better; let it be this evening — here, by the Spring Gardens. We shall scarcely be interrupted.

SIR LUCIUS: *(asserting his paradoxical Irish pride)* Faith! that same interruption in affairs of this nature shows very great ill-breeding. I don't know what's the reason, but in England, if a thing of this kind gets wind, people make such a pother that a gentleman can never fight in peace and quietness. However, if it's the same to you, Captain, I should take it as a particular kindness if you'd let us meet in King's-Mead-Fields, as a little business will call me there about six o'clock, and I may dispatch both matters at once.

CAPTAIN ABSOLUTE: *(offhandedly)* 'Tis the same to me

exactly. A little after six, then, we will discuss this matter more seriously.

SIR LUCIUS: *(with heavy dignity)* If you please, sir, there will be very pretty small-sword light, though it won't do for a long shot. *(bowing stiffly)* So that matter's settled, and my mind's at ease! *(He strides off with dignity to the right walking past Captain Absolute who sees Faulkland coming from the left just as Sir Lucius disappears into the wings.)*

CAPTAIN ABSOLUTE: Well met! I was going to look for you. O Faulkland! all the demons of spite and disappointment have conspired against me! I'm so vexed, that if I had not the prospect of a resource in being knocked o' the head by-and-by, I should scarce have spirits to tell you the cause.

FAULKLAND:*(surprised)* What can you mean? — Has Lydia changed her mind? — I should have thought her duty and inclination would now have pointed to the same object.

CAPTAIN ABSOLUTE: *(with exasperation)* Aye, just as the eyes of a person who squints: when her love-eye was fixed on me, t'other, her eye of duty, was finely obliqued: but when duty bid her point that the same way, off t'other turned on a swivel, and secured its retreat with a frown!

FAULKLAND: *(puzzled by his previous reference to "being knocked o' the head")* But what's the resource you —

CAPTAIN ABSOLUTE: Oh, to wind up the whole, a good-natured Irishman here has — *(mimicking Sir Lucius' brogue)* — begged leave to have the pleasure of cutting my throat; *(crisply)* and I mean to indulge him — that's all.

FAULKLAND: *(incredulous)* Prithee, be serious!

CAPTAIN ABSOLUTE: *(seriously)* 'Tis fact, upon my soul! Sir Lucius O'Trigger — you know him by sight — for some affront, which I am sure I never intended, has obliged me to meet him this evening at six o'clock: 'tis on that account I wished to see you; you must go with me.

FAULKLAND: Nay, there must be some mistake, sure. Sir Lucius shall explain himself, and I dare say matters may be accommodated. *(wrinkling his brow)* But this evening did you say? I wish it had been any other time.

CAPTAIN ABSOLUTE: Why? there will be light enough: — there will, as Sir Lucius says, *(imitating him again)* "be very pretty small-sword light, though it will not do for a long shot." *(with irritation)* Confound his long shots!

FAULKLAND: *(miserably quarrelling with himself)* But I am myself a good deal ruffled by a difference I have had with Julia. My vile tormenting temper has made me treat her so cruelly, that I shall not be myself till we are reconciled.

CAPTAIN ABSOLUTE: *(endlessly amazed at his friend's tortured reactions)* By Heavens! Faulkland, you don't deserve her!

A servant enters from the left, gives Faulkland a letter, and goes out.

FAULKLAND: *(his despair intensified as he recognizes the handwriting on the envelope)* Oh, Jack, this is from Julia. I dread to open it! I fear it may be to take a last leave! — perhaps to bid me return her letters, and restore — Oh, how I suffer for my folly!

CAPTAIN ABSOLUTE: *(encouragingly)* Here, let me see. *(takes the letter, opens it, and glances quickly through it)* Aye, a final sentence, indeed! — 'tis all over with you, faith!

FAULKLAND: *(pleadingly)* Nay, Jack, don't keep me in suspense!

CAPTAIN ABSOLUTE: Hear then. — *(reads)* "As I am convinced that my dear Faulkland's own reflections have already upbraided him for his last unkindness to me, I will not add a word on the subject. I wish to speak with you as soon as possible. Yours ever and truly, Julia." *(heartily)* There's stubbornness and resentment for you! *(giving him the letter)* Why, man, you don't seem one whit the happier at this!

FAULKLAND: *(with a worried frown)* O yes, I am; but — but —

CAPTAIN ABSOLUTE: *(violently)* Confound your buts! — you never hear anything that would make another man bless himself, but you immediately damn it with a but!

FAULKLAND: *(deeply serious and still entangled in his madhouse etiquette of love)* Now, Jack, as you are my friend, own honestly — don't you think there is something forward, something indelicate, in this haste to forgive? Women should never sue for reconciliation: that should always come from us. They should retain their coldness till wooed to kindness; and their pardon, like their love, should "not unsought be won."

CAPTAIN ABSOLUTE: *(bursting out in complete vexation)* I have not patience to listen to you: — thou'rt incorrigible! so say no more on the subject. I must go to settle a few matters. Let me see you before six — remember — at my lodgings. A poor industrious devil like me, who have toiled, and drudged, and plotted to gain my ends, and am at last disappointed by other people's folly, may in pity be allowed to swear and grumble a little; — but a captious sceptic in love, a slave to fretfulness and whim, who has no difficulties but of his own creating, is a subject more fit for ridicule than compassion! *(He strides angrily off into the right wings.)*

FAULKLAND: *(musing to himself as he starts at a very slow gait in the opposite direction)* I feel his reproaches; yet I could not change this too exquisite nicety for the gross content with which he tramples on the thorns of love! His engaging me in this duel has started an idea in my head, which I will instantly pursue. I'll use it as the touchstone of Julia's sincerity and disinterestedness. If her love prove pure and sterling ore, my name will rest on it with honor; and once I've stamped it there, I lay aside my doubts for ever! But if the dross of selfishness, the alloy of pride, predominate, 'twill be best to leave her as a toy for some less cautious fool to sigh for! *(He goes off to the left still groping in the labyrinth of pointless love-analysis.)*

ACT FIVE

Scene One

Julia's Dressing Room. Julia is sitting at her dressing table pondering over a note which she has received from Faulkland.

JULIA: How this message has alarmed me! what dreadful accident can he mean? why such a charge to be *alone?* — O Faulkland! — how many unhappy moments — how many tears have you cost me! *(Faulkland comes in.)* What means this? — why this caution, Faulkland?

FAULKLAND: *(most dramatically)* Alas! Julia, I am come to take a long farewell.

JULIA: *(in grave alarm)* Heavens' what do you mean?

FAULKLAND: You see before you a wretch, whose life is forfeited. *(holding out his hand to prevent the exclamation which Julia seems on the verge of making)* Nay, start not! — the infirmity of my temper has drawn all this misery on me. I left you fretful and passionate — an untoward accident drew me into a quarrel — the event[1] is that I must fly this kingdom instantly. *(soulfully)* O Julia, had I been so fortunate as to have called you mine entirely, before this mischief had fallen on me, I should not so deeply dread my banishment!

JULIA: *(in a glow of love and compassion that lights up the flowering garden of sentimental rhetoric)* My soul is oppressed with sorrow at the nature of your misfortune: had these adverse circumstances arisen from a less fatal cause, I should have felt strong comfort in the thought that I could now chase from your bosom every doubt of the warm sincerity of my love. My heart has

[1] Outcome.

long known no other guardian — I now entrust my person to your honor — we will fly together. When safe from pursuit, my father's will may be fulfilled — and I receive a legal claim to be the partner of your sorrows, and tenderest comforter. Then on the bosom of your wedded Julia, you may lull your keen regret to slumbering; while virtuous love, with a cherub's hand, shall smooth the brow of upbraiding thought, and pluck the thorn from compunction.

FAULKLAND: *(touched but determined to push his test of her love to the limit)* O Julia! I am bankrupt in gratitude! but the time is so pressing, it calls on you for so hasty a resolution! — Would you not wish some hours to weigh the advantages you forego, and what little compassion poor Faulkland can make you besides his solitary love?

JULIA: *(quickly)* I ask not a moment. No, Faulkland, I have loved you for yourself: and if I now, more than ever, prize the solemn engagement which so long has pledged us to each other, it is because it leaves no room for hard aspersions on my fame, and puts the seal of duty to an act of love. *(urgently)* But let us not linger. Perhaps this delay —

FAULKLAND: *(interrupting)* 'Twill be better I should not venture out again till dark. Yet am I grieved to think what numberless distresses will press heavy on your gentle disposition.

JULIA: *(eagerly brushing aside his pretended qualms)* Perhaps your fortune may be forfeited by this unhappy act. I know not whether 'tis so; but sure that alone can never make us unhappy. The little I have will be sufficient to support us; and exile never should be splendid.

FAULKLAND: *(broodingly)* Aye, but in such an abject state of life, my wounded pride perhaps may increase the natural fretfulness of my temper, till I become a rude, morose companion, beyond your patience to endure. Perhaps the recollection of a deed my conscience cannot justify may haunt me in such gloomy and unsocial fits, that I shall hate the tenderness that would relieve me, break from your arms, and quarrel with your fondness!

JULIA: *(tenderly)* If your thoughts should assume so unhappy a bent, you will the more want some mild and affectionate spirit to watch over and console you: one who, by bearing your infirmities with gentleness and resignation, may teach you so to bear the evils of your fortune.

FAULKLAND: *(finally convinced)* Julia, I have proved you to the quick! and with this useless device I throw away all my doubts. *(beseechingly)* How shall I plead to be forgiven this last unworthy effect of my restless, unsatisfied disposition?

JULIA: *(scarcely able to credit her ears)* Has no such disaster happened as you related?

FAULKLAND: *(clearly expecting to be forgiven)* I am ashamed to own that it was pretended; yet in pity, Julia, do not kill me with resenting a fault which never can be repeated: but sealing, this once, my pardon, let me tomorrow, in the face of Heaven, receive my future guide and monitress, and expiate my past folly by years of tender adoration. *(holds out his arms as if to embrace her)*

JULIA: *(tears coming to her eyes as she rejects his arms)* Hold, Faulkland! — that you are free from a crime, which I before feared to name, Heaven knows how sincerely I rejoice! These are tears of thankfulness for that! But that your cruel doubts should have urged you to an imposition that has wrung my heart, gives me now a pang more keen that I can express!

FAULKLAND: *(too introspectively tortured to comprehend what he has done)* By Heavens! Julia —

JULIA: *(still tearful, but interrupting with firmness)* Yet hear me. — My father loved you, Faulkland! and you preserved the life that tender parent gave me; in his presence I pledged my hand — joyfully pledged it — where before I had given my heart. When, soon after, I lost that parent, it seemed to me that Providence had, in Faulkland, shown me whither to transfer without a pause my grateful duty, as well as my affection: hence I have been content to bear from you what pride and delicacy

would have forbid me from another. I will not upbraid
you by repeating how you have trifled with my sincerity —

FAULKLAND: *(earnestly)* I confess it all! yet hear —

JULIA: *(with somber clearsightedness)* After such a
year of trial, I might have flattered myself that I should
not have been insulted with a new probation of my sincerity, as cruel as unnecessary! I now see it is not in your
nature to be content or confident in love. With this conviction — I never will be yours. While I had hopes that
my persevering attention, and unreproaching kindness,
might in time reform your temper, I should have been
happy to have gained a dearer influence over you; but I
will not furnish you with a licensed power to keep alive
an incorrigible fault, at the expense of one who never
would contend with you.

FAULKLAND: *(protesting)* Nay, but, Julia, by my soul
and honor, if after this —

JULIA: *(ignoring his outburst)* But one word more. —
As my faith has once been given to you, I never will bar-
ter it with another. I shall pray for your happiness with
the truest sincerity; and the dearest blessing I can ask of
Heaven to send you, will be to charm you from that unhappy temper, which alone has prevented the performance of our solemn engagement. All I request of you is
that you will yourself reflect upon this infirmity, and
when you number up the many true delights it has de-
prived you of, let it not be your least regret that it lost
you the love of one who would have followed you in
beggary through the world! *(She walks with dignity to the
door at the right and leaves him alone in the room.)*

FAULKLAND: *(stunned)* She's gone! — for ever! —
There was an awful resolution in her manner that riveted
me to my place. — O fool! — dolt — barbarian! Cursed
as I am, with more imperfections than my fellow-
wretches, kind Fortune sent a heaven-gifted cherub to
my aid, and, like a ruffian, I have driven her from my
side! — I must now haste to my appointment. *(bitterly)*
Well, my mind is tuned for such a scene. I shall wish
only to become a principal in it, and reverse the tale my

cursed folly put me upon forging here. *(with an anguished cry)* O Love! — tormentor! — fiend — whose influence, like the moon's acting on men of dull souls, makes idiots of them, but meeting subtler spirits, betrays their course, and urges sensibility to madness! *(He storms out to the left.)*

Julia's maid appears at the back center door escorting Lydia. She looks about the room as if surprised to find it empty.

MAID: My mistress, ma'am, I know, was here just now — perhaps she is only in the next room. *(She goes through the right hand door to seek out Julia.)*

LYDIA: *(musing aloud)* Heigh-ho! Though he has used me so, this fellow runs strangely in my head. I believe one lecture from my grave cousin will make me recall him. *(exclaiming as Julia comes in)* O Julia, I am come to you with such an appetite for consolation. *(pausing suddenly and staring at Julia)* Lud! child, what's the matter with you? You have been crying! — I'll be hanged if that Faulkland has not been tormenting you!

JULIA: *(faintly)* You mistake the cause of my uneasiness! — something has flurried me a little. Nothing that you can guess at. *(aside)* I would not accuse Faulkland to a sister!

LYDIA: *(reassured and preoccupied with her own problem)* Ah! whatever vexations you may have, I can assure you mine surpass them. *(as if about to make an overwhelming revelation)* You know who Beverley proves to be?

JULIA: *(with sisterly solicitude)* I will own to you, Lydia, that Mr. Faulkland had before informed me of the whole affair. *(with a faint trace of self-conscious superiority)* Had young Absolute been the person you took him for, I should not have accepted your confidence on the subject without a serious endeavor to counteract your caprice.

LYDIA: *(crushed)* So, then, I see I have been deceived by everyone! *(pertulantly)* But I don't care — I'll never have him.

JULIA: *(soothingly)* Nay, Lydia —

LYDIA: *(with mounting exasperation)* Why, is it not provoking? when I thought we were coming to the prettiest distress imaginable, to find myself made a mere Smithfield bargain[2] of at last! There had I projected one of the most sentimental elopements! — so becoming a disguise! — so amiable a ladder of ropes! — conscious moon — four horses — Scotch parson — with such surprise to Mrs. Malaprop — and such paragraphs in the newspapers! *(heaving a prodigious sigh)* Oh, I shall die with disappointment!

JULA: *(totally unable to sympathize, remembering her recent offers to Faulkland)* I don't wonder at it!

LYDIA: *(with increasing bitterness)* Now — sad reverse — what have I to expect, but, after a deal of flimsy preparation with a bishop's licence, and my aunt's blessing to go simpering up to the altar; or perhaps be cried three times in a country church, and have an unmannerly fat clerk ask the consent of every butcher in the parish to join John Absolute and Lydia Languish, spinster![3] Oh, that I should live to hear myself called spinster.

JULIA: *(drily)* Melancholy, indeed.

LYDIA: *(so preoccupied with her own woe that she does not notice Julia's lack of sympathy)* How mortifying to remember the dear delicious shifts I used to be put to, to gain half a minute's conversation with this fellow! — How often have I stole forth, in the coldest night in January, and found him in the garden, stuck like a dripping statue! There would he kneel to me in the snow, and sneeze and cough so pathetically! he shivering with cold, and I with apprehension! and while the freezing blast numbed our joints, how warmly would he press me to pity his flame, and glow with mutual ardor *(sighing)* Ah, Julia, that was something like being in love.

---

[2] Marriage for money.

[3] References to the parish ceremonials of announcing approaching nuptials three times from the pulpit, together with the ritualistic statement that any objector to the marriage must then speak "or forever hold his peace."

JULIA: *(somberly)* If I were in spirits, Lydia, I should chide you only by laughing heartily at you; but it suits more the situation of my mind, at present, earnestly to entreat you not to let a man, who loves you with sincerity, suffer that unhappiness from your caprice, which I know too well caprice can inflict.

LYDIA: *(looking toward the door)* O Lud! what has brought my aunt here?

Mrs. Malaprop sweeps in, followed by Fag and David.

MRS. MALAPROP: *(extremely excited)* So! so! here's fine work! — here's fine suicide, parricide, and simulation[4] going on in the fields! and Sir Anthony not to be found to prevent the antistrophe![5]

JULIA: For Heaven's sake, madam, what's the meaning of this?

MRS. MALAPROP: *(pointing at Fag)* That gentleman can tell you — 'twas he enveloped[6] the affair to me.

LYDIA: *(to Fag)* Do, sir, will you, inform us?

FAG: *(speaking slowly and weighing his words)* Ma'am, I should hold myself very deficient in every requisite that forms the man of breeding, if I delayed a moment to give all the information in my power to a lady so deeply interested in the affair as you are.

LYDIA: *(intrigued and impatient)* But quick! quick, sir!

FAG: *(thoughtfully)* True, ma'am, as you say, one should be quick in divulging matters of this nature; for should we be tedious, perhaps while we are flourishing on the subject, two or three lives may be lost!

LYDIA: *(explosively)* O patience! *(to Mrs. Malaprop)* Do, ma'am, for Heaven's sake! tell us what is the matter?

MRS. MALAPROP: *(vehemently)* Why, murder's the matter! slaughter's the matter! killing's the matter! — *(pointing at Fag again)* — But he can tell you the perpendiculars.[7]

---

[4] *Homicide* and *dissimulation?*

[5] Catastrophe.

[6] *Unveiled?*

[7] *Particulars.*

LYDIA: *(in exasperated entreaty to Fag)* Then, prithee, sir, be brief.

FAG: *(with deliberation)* Why, then, ma'am, as to murder — I cannot take upon me to say — and as to slaughter, or manslaughter, that will be as the jury finds it.

LYDIA: But *who*, sir — who are engaged in this?

FAG: *(obligingly)* Faith, ma'am, one is a young gentleman whom I should be very sorry anything was to happen to — a very pretty behaved gentleman! *(reminiscently)* We have lived much together, and always on terms.

LYDIA: *(beside herself with agonized frustration)* But who is this? who? who? who?

FAG: *(as if explaining the obvious)* My master, ma'am — my master — I speak of my master.

LYDIA: *(shocked)* Heavens! What, Captain Absolute!

MRS. MALAPROP: *(pleased with Lydia's concern but with some venom because of her previous intransigence)* Oh, to be sure, you are frightened now!

JULIA: *(deeply interested)* But who are with him, sir?

FAG: *(referring to David)* As to the rest, ma'am, this gentleman can inform you better than I.

JULIA: *(to David)* Do speak, friend.

DAVID: *(excitedly)* Look'ee, my lady — by the mass! there's mischief going on. Folks don't use to meet for amusement with firearms, fire-locks, fire-engines, fire-screens, fire-office, and the devil knows what other crackers beside! — This, my lady I say, has an angry favor.[8]

JULIA: *(fluttering with anticipation that Faulkland is involved)* But who is there beside Captain Absolute, friend?

DAVID: *(gloomily)* My poor master — *(apologetically)* — under favor for mentioning him first. *(explaining his awareness of the niceties of rank)* You know me, my lady — I am David — and my master of course is, or was, Squire Acres. — *Then* comes Squire Faulkland.

JULIA: *(to Mrs. Malaprop)* Do, ma'am, let us instantly endeavor to prevent mischief.

---

[8] Appearance.

MRS. MALAPROP: *(reprovingly)* O fie! — it would be very inelegant in us: — we should only participate[9] things.

DAVID: *(beseechingly to Mrs. Malaprop)* Ah! do, Mrs. Aunt, save a few lives — they are desperately given, believe me. — Above all, there is that bloodthirsty Philistine, Sir Lucius O'Trigger.

MRS. MALAPROP: *(with sudden alarm)* Sir Lucius O'-Trigger? O mercy! have they drawn poor little dear Sir Lucius into the scrape? — *(turning angrily on Lydia)* Why, how you stand, girl! you have no more feeling than one of the Derbyshire putrifactions![10]

LYDIA: *(anxiously)* What are we to do, madam?

MRS. MALAPROP: *(excitedly)* Why, fly with the utmost felicity,[11] to be sure, to prevent mischief! — *(to Fag)* — Here, friend, you can show us the place!

FAG: *(with punctilious dignity)* If you please, ma'am, I will conduct you. — David, do look for Sir Anthony. *(David goes off meekly.)*

MRS. MALAPROP: *(with frantic haste)* Come, girls! this gentleman will exhort[12] us. — *Come,* sir, you're our envoy[13]— lead the way, and we'll precede.[14]

FAG: *(not moving, and bowing low)* Not a step before the ladies for the world!

MRS. MALAPROP: *(nervously as she sweeps by him, pushing the two young ladies before her to the door)* You're sure you know the spot?

FAG: *(following with dignity)* I think I can find it, ma'am; and one good thing is, we shall hear the report of the pistols as we draw ner, so we can't well miss them; — *(with condescending words of comfort as he leaves the stage)* — never fear, ma'am, never fear.

---

[9] *Precipitate.*
[10] Petrified objects found in Derbyshire.
[11] *Facility?*
[12] *Escort.*
[13] *Convoy.*
[14] She means *follow* and is confused with *proceea.*

Scene Two

The South Parade, very much like the North Parade though a trifle more remote from the social centers. Captain Absolute enters from the left looking about him very impatiently. He carries a sword which he seems suddenly to become aware of and carefully conceals it beneath the great-coat he is wearing.

CAPTAIN ABSOLUTE: A sword seen in the streets of Bath[1] would raise as great an alarm as a mad dog. *(looking about anxiously)* How provoking this is in Faulkland! — never punctual! I shall be obligated to go without him at last. *(recognizing his father about to enter from the left)* Oh, here's Sir Anthony! how shall I escape him? *(muffles up his face and swings in a wide circle to the back of the stage as Sir Anthony comes on, seems to recognize his son, and then hesitates as Captain Absolute moves to avoid him)*

SIR ANTHONY: *(thinking aloud)* How one may be deceived at a little distance! only that I see he don't know me, I could have sworn that was Jack! *(peering sharply after him)* Hey! Gad's life! it is. *(calling)* Why, Jack, what are you afraid of; hey! *(to himself)* Sure I'm right. *(shouting)* Why, Jack, Jack Absolute! *(moves rapidly toward him)*

CAPTAIN ABSOLUTE: *(in a disguised voice)* Really, sir, you have the advantage of me: — I don't remember ever to have had the honor — my name is Saunderson, at your service.

SIR ANTHONY: *(apologetically)* Sir, I beg your pardon — I took you — *(catching a glimpse of his face which has been half turned away)* — hey! — why, zounds! it is — Stay — *(pulling him around for a full view of his face)* So, so — your humble servant, Mr. Saunderson! Why, you scoundrel, what tricks are you after now?

---

[1] The prohibition against wearing of swords in Bath originated during the regime of Beau Nash.

CAPTAIN ABSOLUTE: *(lightly)* Oh, a joke, sir, a joke! I came here on purpose to look for you, sir.

SIR ANTHONY: *(skeptically)* You did! well I am glad you were so lucky: — but what are you muffled up so for? — what's this for? — hey?

CAPTAIN ABSOLUTE: *(nervously)* 'Tis cool, sir, isn't it? — rather chilly somehow: — but I shall be late — I have a particular engagement.

SIR ANTHONY: *(peremptorily)* Stay! — Why, I thought you were looking for me? — Pray, Jack, where is't you are going?

CAPTAIN ABSOLUTE: *(completely flustered)* Going, sir?

SIR ANTHONY: *(shouting)* Aye, where are you going?

CAPTAIN ABSOLUTE: *(helplessly)* Where am I going?

SIR ANTHONY: *(raging)* You unmannerly puppy!

CAPTAIN ABSOLUTE: *(attempting to recover)* I was going, sir, to — to — to — to *Lydia* — *(gaining confidence)* — sir, to Lydia — to make matters up if I could; — and I was looking for you, sir, *(lost again)* to — to —

SIR ANTHONY: *(heartily)* To go with you, I suppose. — Well, come along.

CAPTAIN ABSOLUTE: *(exclaiming)* Oh! zounds, no, sir, not for the world! *(again fumbling to extricate himself)* I wished to meet with you, sir, — to — to — to — *(with sudden solicitude)* You find it cool, I'm sure, sir — you'd better not stay out.

SIR ANTHONY: *(attributing his son's odd behavior to shyness and determined to encourage him)* Cool! — not at all. Well, Jack — and what will you say to Lydia?

CAPTAIN ABSOLUTE: *(thoughtfully)* Oh, sir, beg her pardon, humor her — promise and vow: but I detain you, sir — consider the cold air on your gout.

SIR ANTHONY: *(in high good humor)* Oh, not at all! — not at all! I'm in no hurry. *(shaking his head indulgently)* Ah! Jack, you youngsters, when once you are wounded here — *(putting his hand over his son's heart)* Hey! what the deuce have you got here?

CAPTAIN ABSOLUTE: *(in great confusion, attempting to pull away)* Nothing, sir — nothing.

SIR ANTHONY: *(continuing to explore with his hand)* What's this? — here's something hard.

CAPTAIN ABSOLUTE: *(faintly)* Oh, trinkets, sir! trinkets! — a bauble for Lydia!

SIR ANTHONY: Nay, let me see your taste. *(pulls his coat open, whereat the sword falls clattering to the stage)* Trinkets! — bauble for Lydia! — zounds! sirrah, you are not going to cut her throat, are you?

CAPTAIN ABSOLUTE: *(hollowly)* Ha! ha! ha! — I thought it would divert you, sir, though I didn't mean to tell you till afterwards.

SIR ANTHONY: *(picking up the sword)* You didn't? — Yes, this is a diverting trinket, truly! *(returning it to his son)*

CAPTAIN ABSOLUTE: *(with sudden inspiration)* Sir, I'll explain to you. You know, sir, Lydia is romantic, devilish romantic, and very absurd of course: now, sir, I intend, if she refuses to forgive me, to unsheath this sword, and swear I'll fall upon its point, and expire at her feet!

SIR ANTHONY: *(disgusted)* Fall upon a fiddlestick's end! *(slowly catching the idea)* Why, I suppose it *is* the very thing that would please her. *(laughing)* Get along, you fool!

CAPTAIN ABSOLUTE: *(relieved)* Well, sir, you shall hear of my success — you shall hear. *(striking a dramatic pose)* "O Lydia! — forgive me, or this pointed steel —" says I.

SIR ANTHONY: *(with great good humor)* "O, booby! stab away and welcome," says she. *(laughing and slapping him on the shoulder)* Get along!

Captain Absolute exits hurriedly to the left as his father indulgently follows his departure with his eyes. Suddenly, David erupts on to the stage from the right.

DAVID: *(at the top of his lungs)* Stop him! stop him! Murder! Thief! Fire! Stop fire! Stop fire! *(breathlessly)*

O Sir Anthony — call! call! bid'm stop! *(his voice breaking with exhaustion)* Murder! Fire!

SIR ANTHONY: *(with puzzled deliberateness)* Fire! Murder! — Where?

DAVIDS *(collapsing)* Oons! he's out of sight, and I'm out of breath, for my part! *(pleadingly)* O Sir Anthony, why didn't you stop him? why didn't you stop him?

SIR ANTHONY: Zounds! the fellow's mad! — stop whom! stop Jack?

DAVID: *(eagerly)* Aye, the captain, sir! — there's murder and slaughter —

SIR ANTHONY: *(with an exclamation of great concern)* Murder!

DAVID: *(his words tumbling on one another)* Aye, please you, Sir Anthony, there's all kinds of murder, all sorts of slaughter to be seen in the fields: there's fighting going on, sir — bloody sword-and-gun fighting!

SIR ANTHONY: *(looking as if he would like to trounce him)* Who are going to fight, dunce?

DAVID: *(still hysterical with excitement)* Everybody that I know of, Sir Anthony: — everybody is going to fight: my poor master, Sir Lucius O'Trigger, your son, the Captain —

SIR ANTHONY: *(the light breaking)* Oh, the dog! I see his tricks. — Do you know the place?

DAVID: King's-Mead-Fields.

SIR ANTHONY: *(sharply)* You know the way?

DAVID: Not an inch; but I'll call the mayor — aldermen — constables — church-wardens — and beadles — we can't be too many to part them.

SIR ANTHONY: *(annoyed, concerned, and with mounting anger)* Come along — give me your shoulder! we'll get assistance as we go — the lying villain! — Well, I shall be in such a frenzy! — so — this was the history of his trinkets! *(shouting as he forces David off stage to the left with him)* I'll baubel him!

Scene Three

*King's-Mead-Fields, a spacious isolated field stretching
from King's-Mead House to the river. Sir Lucius O'Trigger and Bob Acres, both equipped with pistols, stroll on
from the right. Acres is not at all sure that he is enthusiastic about the approaching encounter. Sir Lucius is entirely unsympathetic and full of hearty anticipation.*

ACRES: *(protesting vehemently)* By my valor! then,
Sir Lucius, forty yards is a good distance. Odds levels
and aims! — I say it is a good distance.

SIR LUCIUS: *(scornfully)* Is it for muskets or small
field pieces! Upon my conscience, Mr. Acres, you must
leave those things to me. Stay now — I'll show you
(paces off a short distance across the stage) There now,
that is a very pretty distance — a pretty gentleman's
distance.

ACRES: Zounds! we might as well fight in a sentry-box!
(attempting to reason with him) I tell you, Sir Lucius, the
farther he is off, the cooler I shall take my aim.

SIR LUCIUS: *(with heavy sarcasm)* Faith! then I suppose you would aim at him best of all if he was out of
sight!

ACRES: *(thoughtfully)* No, Sir Lucius; but I should
think forty or eight-and-thirty yards —

SIR LUCIUS: *(interrupting noisily)* Pho! pho! nonsense!
three or four feet between the mouths of your pistols is
as good as a mile.

ACRES: *(emphatically)* Odds bullets, no! — by my
valor! there is no merit in killing him so near. *(pleadingly)* Do, my dear Sir Lucius, let me bring him down at a
long shot: — a long shot, Sir Lucius, if you love me!

SIR LUCIUS: *(brushing aside his plea off-handedly)* Well,
the gentleman's friend and I must settle that. *(gravely)*
But tell me now, Mr. Acres, in case of an accident, is
there any little will or commission I could execute for you?

ACRES: *(faintly)* I am much obliged to you, Sir Lucius,
but I don't understand —

SIR LUCIUS: *(heartily)* Why, you may think there's no being shot at without a little risk — and if an unlucky bullet should carry a quietus[1] with it — I say it will be no time then to be bothering you about family matters.

ACRES: *(gasping)* A quietus!

SIR LUCIUS: *(matter-of-factly)* For instance, now — if that should be the case — would you choose to be pickled and sent home? — or would it be the same to you to lie here in the Abbey? I'm told there is very snug lying in the Abbey.[2]

ACRES: *(aghast)* Pickled! — snug lying in the Abbey! — Odds tremors! Sir Lucius, don't talk so!

SIR LUCIUS: *(casually)* I suppose, Mr. Acres, you never were engaged in an affair of this kind before?

ACRES: *(apologetically)* No, Sir Lucius, never before.

SIR LUCIUS: *(sympathetically)* Ah! that's a pity! — there's nothing like being used to a thing. *(as if questioning a pupil)* Pray now, how would you receive the gentleman's shot?

ACRES: *(enthusiastically)* Odds files! — I've practised that — *(strikes an attitude)* — there, Sir Lucius — there. A side-front, hey? Odd! I'll make myself small enough: I'll stand edgeways.

SIR LUCIUS: *(with gentle superiority)* Now — you're quite out — for if you stand so when I take my aim — *(draws a pistol and levels it at him)*

ACRES: *(panicky)* Zounds! Sir Lucius — are you sure it is not cocked?

SIR LUCIUS: *(waving the pistol casually as if it were a toy)* Never fear.

ACRES: *(terrified)* But — but — you don't know — it may go off of its own head!

SIR LUCIUS: *(condescendingly)* Pho! be easy. *(in a scientific tone)* Well, now if I hit you in the body, my bullet has a double chance — for if it misses a vital part

---

[1] A discharge or release from life.

[2] A contemporary allusion to the scandalous sanitary conditions prevalent at Bath Abbey at the time.

of your right side — 'twill be very hard if it don't succeed on the left!

ACRES: *(scarcely able to speak)* A vital part!

SIR LUCIUS: *(in the manner of a technical expert going up to Acres, grasping him by the shoulders, and turning him half around as he speaks so that he exposes his full front to his opponent)* But there — fix yourself so — let him see the broadside of your full front — there — now a ball or two may pass clean through your body, and never do any harm at all.

ACRES: *(gasping)* Clean through me! — a ball or two clean through me!

SIR LUCIUS: *(enthusiastically)* Aye, may they — and it is much the *genteelest* attitude into the bargain.

ACRES: *(asserting himself)* Look'ee! Sir Lucius — I'd just as lieve be shot in an awkward posture as a genteel one; so by my valor! I will stand edgeways.

SIR LUCIUS: *(looking at his watch)* Sure they don't mean to disappoint us. *(raising his eyes and seeming to see figures approaching from the right)* Hah! — no, faith — I think I see them coming.

ACRES: *(all but inarticulate)* Hey! — what! — coming! —

SIR LUCIUS: *(with enormous satisfaction)* Aye. who are those yonder getting over the stile?

ACRES: *(almost whispering)* There are two of them indeed! *(with hysterical bravado)* Well — let them come — hey, Sir Lucius! — we — we — we — we — won't run.

SIR LUCIUS: *(with violent outrage)* Run!

ACRES: *(forcing himself to find voice)* No — I say — we won't run, by my valor!

SIR LUCIUS: *(sternly)* What the devil's the matter with you?

ACRES: *(faintly)* Nothing — my dear friend — my dear Sir Lucius — but I — I — I don't feel quite so bold, somehow, as I did.

SIR LUCIUS: O fie — consider your honor.

ACRES: *(meekly)* Aye — true — my honor. Do, Sir

Lucius, edge in a word or two every now and then about my honor.

SIR LUCIUS: *(looking off to the left)* Well, here they're coming.

ACRES: *(tremulously)* Sir Lucius — if I wa'n't with you, I should almost think I was afraid. — If my valor should leave me! — Valor *will* come and go.

SIR LUCIUS: *(brusquely)* Then pray keep it fast, while you have it.

ACRES: *(visibly trembling)* Sir Lucius — I doubt[3] it is going — yes — my valor is certainly going! — it is sneaking off! *(holding out his trembling hands)* I feel it oozing out as it were at the palms of my hands!

SIR LUCIUS: *(spiritedly)* Your honor — your honor! — Here they are. *(looking offstage)*

ACRES: *(shaking and gasping)* O mercy! — now — that I was safe at Clod Hall! or could be shot before I was aware!

Captain Absolute and Faulkland appear at the edge of the stage approaching slowly.

SIR LUCIUS: *(bowing with great formality)* Gentlemen, your most obedient. *(recognizing Captain Absolute)* Hah! — what, Captain Absolute! — So, I suppose, sir, you are come here, just like myself — to do a kind office, first for your friend — then to proceed to business on your own account.

ACRES: *(enormously relieved and eagerly greeting a friend)* What, Jack! — my *dear* Jack! — my *dear* friend!

CAPTAIN ABSOLUTE: *(ominously)* Hark'ee, Bob, Beverley's at hand.

SIR LUCIUS: *(rather mystified)* Well, Mr. Acres — I don't blame your saluting the gentleman civilly. *(to Faulkland)* So, Mr. Beverley, if you'll choose your weapons, the Captain and I will measure the ground.

FAULKLAND: *My* weapons, sir!

ACRES: *(exclaiming)* Odds life! Sir Lucius, I'm not going to fight Mr. Faulkland; these are my particular friends.

---

[3] *I think* or *I fear.*

SIR LUCIUS: *(baffled)* What, sir, did you not come to fight Mr. Acres?

FAULKLAND: Not I, upon my word, sir.

SIR LUCIUS: *(annoyed)* Well, now, that's mighty provoking! But I hope, Mr. Faulkland, as there are three of us come on purpose for the game, you won't be so cantankerous as to spoil the party by sitting out.

CAPTAIN ABSOLUTE: *(with mock anxiety)* O pray, Faulkland, fight to oblige Sir Lucius.

FAULKLAND: *(joining the fun)* Nay, if Mr. Acres is so bent on the matter —

ACRES: *(interrupting hastily)* No, no, Mr. Faulkland; I'll bear my disappointment like a Christian. — Look'ee, Sir Lucius, there's no occasion at all for me to fight; and if it is the same to you, I'd as lieve let it alone.

SIR LUCIUS: *(sternly)* Observe me, Mr. Acres — I must not be trifled with. You have certainly challenged somebody — and you came here to fight him. Now, if that gentleman is willing to represent him *(pointing at Faulkland),* I can't see, for my soul, why it isn't the same thing.

ACRES: *(insistent*ly*)* Why no — Sir Lucius — I tell you, 'tis one Beverley I've challenged — *(with a swagger)* — a fellow, you see, that dare not show his face! If he were here, I'd make him give up his pretensions directly.

CAPTAIN ABSOLUTE: *(with clipped precision)* Hold, Bob — let me set you right — there is no such man as Beverley in the case. The person who assumed that name is before you; and as his pretensions are the same in both characters, he is ready to support them in whatever way you please.

SIR LUCIUS: *(his face lighting up)* Well, this is lucky. — Now you have an opportunity —

ACRES: *(hastily)* What, quarrel with my dear friend, Jack Absolute? *(emphatically)* Not if he were fifty Beverleys! Zounds! Sir Lucius, you would not have me so unnatural.

SIR LUCIUS: *(chagrined)* Upon my conscience, Mr. Acres, your valor has oozed away with a vengeance!

ACRES: *(his valor reviving rapidly)* Not in the least! Odds backs and abettors! I'll be your second with all my heart — and if you should get a quietus, you may command me entirely. I'll get you snug lying in the Abbey here; or pickle you, and send you over to Blunderbuss Hall, or anything of the kind, with the greatest pleasure.

SIR LUCIUS: *(disgusted)* Pho! pho! you are little better than a coward.

ACRES: *(bridling)* Mind, gentlemen, he calls me a coward; coward was the word, by my valor.

SIR LUCIUS: *(with stiff dignity)* Well, sir?

ACRES: *(reasonably)* Look'ee, Sir Lucius, 'tisn't that I mind the word coward — coward may be said in joke — *(noisily)* — but if you had called me a poltroon, odds daggers and balls —

SIR LUCIUS: *(in the identical tone of voice as before)* Well, sir?

ACRES: *(fading)* I should have thought you a very ill-bred man.

SIR LUCIUS: *(scornfully)* Pho! you are beneath my notice.

CAPTAIN ABSOLUTE: *(with gusto)* Nay, Sir Lucius, you can't have a better second than my friend Acres. He is a most determined dog — called in the country, "Fighting Bob." He generally kills a man a week — don't you, Bob?

ACRES: *(shamefacedly)* Aye — at home.

SIR LUCIUS: Well, then, Captain, 'tis *we* must begin — *(drawing his sword)* — so come out, my little counsellor and ask the gentleman whether he will resign the lady without forcing you to proceed against him?

CAPTAIN ABSOLUTE: *(a trifly wearily)* Come on then, sir. *(drawing his sword)* Since you won't let it be an amicable suit, here's my reply.

At this moment there burst into the scene Sir Anthony Absolute and David, followed by Mrs. Malaprop, Lydia, and Julia.

DAVID: *(panicky)* Knock 'em all down, sweet Sir Anthony; knock down my master in particular; and bind his hand over to their good behavior! *(The duelists pause.)*

SIR ANTHONY: *(roaring)* Put up, Jack, put up, or I shall be in a frenzy — how came you in a duel, sir?

CAPTAIN ABSOLUTE: *(mildly)* Faith, sir, that gentleman can tell you better than I; 'twas he called on me, and you know, sir, I serve his Majesty.

SIR ANTHONY: *(grimly)* Here's a pretty fellow; I catch him going to cut a man's throat, and he tells me he serves his majesty! *(shouting)* Zounds! sirrah, then how durst you draw the king's sword against one of his subjects?

CAPTAIN ABSOLUTE: *(insistently)* Sir, I tell you! that gentleman called me out, without explaining his reasons.

SIR ANTHONY: *(exploding at Sir Lucius)* Gad! sir, how came you to call my son out, without explaining your reasons?

SIR LUCIUS: *(coldly)* Your son, sir, insulted me in a manner which my honor could not brook.

SIR ANTHONY: *(with increased fury)* Zounds! Jack, how durst you insult the gentleman in a manner which his honor could not brook?

MRS. MALAPROP: *(fluttering)* Come, come, let's have no honor before ladies. Captain Absolute, come here. How could you intimidate us so? Here's Lydia has been terrified to death for you.

CAPTAIN ABSOLUTE: *(with a grimace)* For fear I should be killed, or escape, ma'am?

MRS. MALAPROP: *(shaking her finger at him as if to a naughty child)* Nay, no delusions[4] to the past. *(turning to Lydia)* Lydia is convinced; speak child.

SIR LUCIUS: *(with heavy dignity)* With your leave ma'am, I must put in a word here: I believe I could interpret the young lady's silence. *(leering at Lydia)* Now mark —

LYDIA: *(outraged)* What is it you mean, sir?

SIR LUCIUS: *(with easy confidence)* Come, come, Delia, we must be serious now — this is no time for trifling.

LYDIA: *(soberly)* 'Tis true, sir; *(turning to Captain Ab-*

---

[4] *Allusions.*

solute) and your reproof bids me offer this gentleman my hand, and solicit the return of his affections.

CAPTAIN ABSOLUTE: *(with grateful warmth)* O! my little angel, say you so? *(firmly to Sir Lucius)* Sir Lucius — I perceive there must be some mistake here, with regard to the affront which you affirm I have given you. I can only say that it could not have been intentional. And as you must be convinced that I should not fear to support a real injury, you shall now see that I am not ashamed to atone for an inadvertency — I ask your pardon. *(proudly)* But for this lady, while honored with her approbation, I will support any claim against any man whatever.

SIR ANTHONY: *(with heartfelt approval)* Well said, Jack, and I'll stand by you, my boy.

ACRES: *(intruding anxiously)* Mind, I give up all my claim — I make no pretensions to anything in the world; and if I can't get a wife without fighting for her, by my valor! I'll live a bachelor.

SIR LUCIUS: *(thoroughly appeased and holding out his hand)* Captain, give me your hand: an affront handsomely acknowledge becomes an obligation; and as for the lady, if she chooses to deny her own handwriting, here — *(pulls a packet of letters from his pocket)*

MRS. MALAPROP: *(with a nervous giggle)* O, he will dissolve⁵ my mystery! — Sir Lucius, perhaps there's some mistake — perhaps I can illuminate —⁶

SIR LUCIUS: *(brushing her aside)* Pray, old gentlewoman, don't interfere where you have no business. *(to Lydia)* Miss Languish, are you my Delia, or not?

LYDIA: *(very exactly as she puts her arm through Captain Absolute's and leads him off to the back of the stage)* Indeed, Sir Lucius, I am not.

MRS. MALAPROP: *(blushing and beaming at the same time)* Sir Lucius O'Trigger — ungrateful as you are — I own the soft impeachment — pardon my blushes, I am Delia.

---

⁵ *Solve.*

⁶ *Elucidate.*

SIR LUCIUS: *(as if responding to a poor joke)* You Delia — pho! pho! be easy.

MRS. MALAPROP: *(insulted)* Why, thou barbarous Van-dyke[7] — those letters are mine. When you are more sensible of my benignity — perhaps I may be brought to encourage your addresses.

SIR LUCIUS: *(with exaggerated politeness)* Mrs. Malaprop, I am extremely sensible of your condescension; and whether you or Lucy have put this trick on me, I am equally beholden to you. *(raising his voice and addressing Captain Absolute)* And to show you I am not ungrateful, Captain Absolute, since you have taken that lady from me, I'll give you my Delia into the bargain.

CAPTAIN ABSOLUTE: *(interrupting his private tête-à-tête with Lydia to reply)* I am much obliged to you, Sir Lucius; but here's my friend, Fighting Bob, unprovided for.

SIR LUCIUS: *(to Acres)* Hah! little Valor — here, will you make your fortune?

ACRES: *(emphatically)* Odds wrinkles! No. — But give me your hand, Sir Lucius, forget and forgive; but if I ever give you a chance of pickling me again, say Bob Acres is a dunce, that's all.

SIR ANTHONY: *(cheerily)* Come, Mrs. Malaprop, don't be cast down — you are in your bloom yet. *(He offers his arm gallantly to lead her off to a private conversation.*

MRS. MALAPROP: *(simpering as she takes his arm)* O Sir Anthony — men are all barbarians.

Sir Anthony leads Mrs. Malaprop to the back of the stage somewhat apart from Captain Absolute and Lydia. Sir Lucius, Bob Acres, and David congregate privately off to the left, leaving Faulkland and Julia alone at the front of the stage.

JULIA: *(glancing surreptitiously at Faulkland, who seems to be making an effort to speak, and voicing her own inner thoughts)* He seems dejected and unhappy — not sullen; there was some foundation, however, for the

---

[7] *Vandal?*

Why, thou barbarous Vandyke———those letters are mine.

tale he told me — O woman! how true should be your judgment, when your resolution is so weak!

FAULKLAND: *(summoning all his courage)* Julia! — how can I sue for what I so little deserve? I dare not presume — yet Hope is the child of Penitence.

JULIA: *(meltingly)* O! Faulkland, you have not been more faulty in your unkind treatment of me than I am now in wanting inclination to resent it. As my heart honestly bids me place my weakness to the account of love, I should be ungenerous not to admit the same plea for yours.

FAULKLAND: *(ecstatically)* Now I shall be blest indeed!

SIR ANTHONY: *(coming forward and noisily interrupting)* What's going on here? — So you have been quarrelling too, I warrant! Come, Julia, I never interfered before; but let me have a hand in the matter at last. *(moderating his tone)* All the faults I have ever seen in my friend Faulkland seemed to proceed from what he calls the delicacy and warmth of his affection for you. *(heartily)* There, marry him directly, Julia; you'll find he'll mend surprisingly! *(aroused by Sir Anthony's noisy outburst from their private conversations, the others come forward with interest.)*

SIR LUCIUS: *(to Julia)* Come, now, I hope there is no dissatisfied person, but what is content; for as I have been disappointed myself, it will be very hard if I have not the satisfaction of seeing other people succeed better.

ACRES: *(good-humoredly)* You are right, Sir Lucius. — So Jack, I wish you joy. Mr. Faulkland, the same. *(with increasing high spirits)* Ladies, — come now, to show you I'm neither vexed nor angry, odds tabors and pipes! I'll order the fiddles in half an hour to the New Rooms — and I insist on your all meeting me there.

SIR ANTHONY: *(responding in kind)* Gad! sir, I like your spirit; and at night we single lads will drink a health to the young couples, and a husband to Mrs. Malaprop. *(During the last two speeches Lydia and Julia have drawn apart in private conversation.)*

FAULKLAND: *(noticing the withdrawal of the girls; to*

Captain Absolute) Our partners are stolen from us, Jack — I hope to be congratulated by each other — yours for having checked in time the errors of an ill-directed imagination, which might have betrayed an innocent heart; and mine for having, by her gentleness and candor, reformed the unhappy temper of one, who by it made wretched whom he loved most, and tortured the heart he ought to have adored.

CAPTAIN ABSOLUTE: *(meditatively)* Well, Faulkland, we have both tasted the bitters, as well as the sweets of love; with this difference only, that you always prepared the bitter cup for yourself, while I —

LYDIA: *(interrupting sharply and returning to the group, Julia following)* Was always obliged to me for it, hey! Mr. Modesty? *(gaily)* But, come, no more of that — our happiness is now as unalloyed as general.

JULIA: *(devoutly)* Then let us study to preserve it so: and while Hope pictures to us a flattering scene of future bliss, let us deny its pencil those colors which are too bright to be lasting. When hearts deserving happiness would unite their fortunes, Virtue would crown them with an unfading garland of modest, hurtless flowers; but ill-judging Passion will force the gaudier rose into the wreath, whose thorn offends them when its leaves are dropped!

They all go off together.

EPILOGUE

Spoken by Julia

Ladies, for you — I heard our poet say —
He'd try to coax some moral from his play:[1]
"One moral's plain," cried I, "without more fuss;
Man's social happiness all rests on us:
Through all the drama — whether damned or not —
Love gilds the scene, and women guide the plot.
From every rank obedience is our due —
D'ye doubt? — The world's great stage shall prove it true."

The CIT,[2] well skilled to shun domestic strife
Will sup abroad; but first he'll ask his wife:
John Trot,[3] his friend, for once will do the same,
But then — he'll just step home to tell his dame.

The surly SQUIRE at noon resolves to rule,
And half the day — Zounds! madam is a fool!
Convinced at night, the vanquished victor says,
"Ah, Kate! you women have such coaxing ways!"

The jolly TOPER chides each tardy blade,
Till reeling Bacchus calls on Love for aid:
Then with each toast he sees fair bumpers swim,
And kisses Chloe on the sparkling brim!

Nay, I have heard that STATESMEN — great and
　　　wise —
Will sometimes counsel with a lady's eyes!
The servile suitors watch her various face,
She smiles preferment, or she frowns disgrace,
Curtsies a pension here — there nods a place.

Nor with less awe, in scenes of humbler life,
Is viewed the mistress, or is heard the wife.

---

[1] Further allusion to the theory of sentimental comedy: that it should guide and edify.

[2] Citizen.

[3] An eighteenth century appellation for an awkward person.

The poorest peasant of the poorest soil,
The child of poverty, and heir to toil,
Early from radiant Love's impartial light
Steals one small spark to cheer this world of night:
Dear spark! that oft through winter's chilling woes
Is all the warmth his little cottage knows!

The wandering TAR, who not for years has pressed
The widowed partner of his day of rest,
On the cold deck, far from her arms removed,
Still hums the ditty which his Susan loved;
And while around the cadence rude is blown,
The boatswain whistles in a softer tone.

The SOLDIER, fairly proud of wounds and toil,
Pants for the triumph of his Nancy's smile;
But ere the battle should he list her cries,
The lover trembles — and the hero dies!
That heart, by war and honor steeled to fear,
Droops on a sigh, and sickens at a tear!

But ye more cautious, ye nice-judging few,
Who give to beauty only beauty's due,
Though friends to love — ye view with deep regret
Our conquests marred, our triumphs incomplete,
Till polished wit more lasting charms disclose,
And judgment fix the darts which beauty throws!
In female breasts did sense and merit rule,
The lover's mind would ask no other school;
Shamed into sense, the scholars of our eyes,
Our beaux from gallantry would soon be wise;
Would gladly light, their homage to improve,
The lamp of knowledge at the torch of love!

BIBLIOGRAPHY

THE PLAYWRIGHT

W. A. Darlington, *Sheridan*. London: Duckworth, 1933.

Kenelm Foss, *Here Lies Richard Brinsley Sheridan*. London: M. Secker, 1939.

Lewis Gibbs (pseudonym of Joseph Walter Cove), *Sheridan*. London: J. M. Dent, 1947.

Alice Glasgow, *Sheridan of Drury Lane*. New York: Frederick A. Stokes Co., 1940.

Raymond C. Rhodes, *Harlequin Sheridan*. Oxford: B. Blackwell, 1933.

THE PLAY

The Dramatic Works of Richard Brinsley Sheridan, introduction by Joseph Knight. Oxford and New York: Oxford University Press, H. Milford, 1930.

Major Dramas of Richard Brinsley Sheridan, introduction and notes by George Henry Nettleton. Boston and London: Ginn & Co., 1906.

The Plays and Poems of Richard Brinsley Sheridan, edited by R. Crompton Rhodes, 3 vols. Oxford: Basil Blackwood, 1928; New York: The Macmillan Co., 1929.

The Rivals, edited by Richard Little Purdy, text of the Larpent ms. and of the first edition, London, 1775, in parallel columns. Oxford: Clarendon Press, 1935.

THE STAGING

Allardyce Nicoll, *The Development of the Theatre*. London: G. G. Harrop & Co., 1937.

Richard Southern, *Changeable Scenery, Its Origin and Development in the English Theatre*. London: Faber and Faber, 1951.